M000072849

THE NEW
POTLUCK

A FRESH TAKE ON CLASSIC FOODS TO SHARE

Publications International, Ltd.

Copyright © 2019 Publications International, Ltd.
All rights reserved. This publication may not be reproduced or quoted in whole or in part by any means whatsoever without written permission from:

Louis Weber, CEO
Publications International, Ltd.
8140 Lehigh Ave
Morton Grove, IL 60053

Permission is never granted for commercial purposes.

All recipes that contain specific brand names are copyrighted by those companies and/or associations, unless otherwise specified. All other recipes and all photographs *except* those on pages 7, 12, 24, 58, 67, 82, 105, 136, 137, 142 and 147 copyright © Publications International, Ltd.

Campbell's® and Swanson® are registered trademarks of CSC Brands LP. All rights reserved.

Pepperidge Farm® is a registered trademark of Pepperidge Farm, Incorporated. All rights reserved.

Some of the products listed in this publication may be in limited distribution.

Pictured on the front cover: Chicken Waldorf Salad *(page 96).*
Pictured on the back cover *(clockwise from top left):* Rich and Gooey Cinnamon Buns *(page 26),* Buffalo Wings *(page 48),* Apple and Carrot Casserole *(page 131),* House Salad *(page 70),* Rainbow Poke Cake *(page 166) and* Truffle Macaroni and Cheese *(page 138).*

ISBN: 978-1-64030-726-1

Manufactured in China.

8 7 6 5 4 3 2 1

WARNING: Food preparation, baking and cooking involve inherent dangers: misuse of electric products, sharp electric tools, boiling water, hot stoves, allergic reactions, foodborne illnesses and the like, pose numerous potential risks. Publications International, Ltd. (PIL) assumes no responsibility or liability for any damages you may experience as a result of following recipes, instructions, tips or advice in this publication.

While we hope this publication helps you find new ways to eat delicious foods, you may not always achieve the results desired due to variations in ingredients, cooking temperatures, typos, errors, omissions, or individual cooking abilities.

Let's get social!
 @Publications_International
 @PublicationsInternational
www.pilcookbooks.com

CONTENTS

BREAKFAST & BRUNCH

CINNAMON-SUGAR CAKE DONUT WAFFLES

MAKES 6 SERVINGS

¾ **cup sugar**

2 **teaspoons ground cinnamon**

1½ **teaspoons ground nutmeg**

1¼ **cups all-purpose flour**

½ **cup whole wheat flour**

2 **teaspoons baking powder**

½ **teaspoon salt**

1¾ **cups buttermilk**

2 **eggs**

6 **tablespoons unsalted butter, melted and slightly cooled**

1½ **teaspoons vanilla**

1. Preheat waffle maker to medium-high heat. Place wire rack on top of large baking sheet.

2. Combine sugar, cinnamon and nutmeg in small bowl. Set aside ½ cup sugar mixture in large bowl; place remainder in large resealable food storage bag.

3. Add flours, baking powder and salt to ½ cup sugar mixture in large bowl. Combine buttermilk, eggs, butter and vanilla in small bowl; stir into dry ingredients just until blended.

4. Place scant ¾ cup batter in center of waffle maker. Close lid and cook 3 to 5 minutes or until waffle is golden brown. Remove waffle and place in storage bag; seal and shake until evenly coated. Remove to wire rack; keep warm. Repeat with remaining batter.

HAM AND ASPARAGUS STRATA

MAKES 8 SERVINGS

4 cups **PEPPERIDGE FARM®
   Cubed Country Style
   Stuffing**

2 cups shredded Swiss cheese
   (about 8 ounces)

1½ cups cooked cut asparagus

1½ cups cubed cooked ham

1 can (10¾ ounces)
   CAMPBELL'S® Condensed
   Cream of Asparagus Soup
   OR **Condensed Cream of
   Mushroom Soup**

2 cups milk

5 eggs

1 tablespoon Dijon-style
   mustard

1. Heat the oven to 350°F. Stir the stuffing, cheese, asparagus and ham in a greased 3-quart shallow baking dish.

2. Beat the soup, milk, eggs and mustard in a medium bowl with a fork or whisk. Pour over the stuffing mixture. Stir and press the stuffing mixture into the milk mixture to coat.

3. Bake for 45 minutes or until a knife inserted in the center comes out clean. Let stand for 5 minutes.

Kitchen Tip: For **1½ CUPS** cooked cut asparagus, use **¾ POUND** fresh asparagus, trimmed and cut into 1-inch pieces **OR 1 PACKAGE** (about 10 ounces) frozen asparagus spears, thawed, drained and cut into 1-inch pieces.

BLUEBERRY CINNAMON MUFFINS

MAKES 12 MUFFINS

1¼ cups all-purpose flour

½ cup **CREAM OF WHEAT®
Cinnamon Swirl Instant
Hot Cereal, uncooked**

½ **cup sugar, divided**

1 **tablespoon baking powder**

2 **teaspoons ground cinnamon**

½ **teaspoon salt**

1 **cup fat-free milk**

1 **egg**

2 **tablespoons oil**

1 **teaspoon vanilla extract**

1 **cup fresh or frozen
blueberries**

2 **tablespoons apple juice**

1. Preheat oven to 400°F. Grease 12 standard (2½-inch) muffin cups. Mix flour, Cream of Wheat, ¼ cup sugar, baking powder, cinnamon and salt in medium bowl; set aside.

2. Beat milk, egg, oil and vanilla with wire whisk in separate bowl until well blended. Add to dry ingredients; stir just until moistened. Gently stir in blueberries. Spoon evenly into prepared muffin cups, filling each cup two-thirds full.

3. Bake 18 to 20 minutes or until toothpick inserted into centers comes out clean. Remove muffins from pan.

4. Brush tops of warm muffins with apple juice; roll in remaining ¼ cup sugar. Serve warm.

Variation: Use CREAM OF WHEAT® Strawberries 'n Cream Instant Hot Cereal and frozen strawberries to make Strawberries 'n Cream Muffins.

BAKED PUMPKIN OATMEAL

MAKES 6 SERVINGS

2 cups old-fashioned oats

2 cups milk

1 cup canned pumpkin

2 eggs

⅓ cup packed brown sugar

1 teaspoon vanilla

½ cup dried cranberries, plus additional for topping

1 teaspoon pumpkin pie spice

½ teaspoon salt

½ teaspoon baking powder

Maple syrup

Chopped pecans (optional)

1. Preheat oven to 350°F. Spray 8-inch square baking dish with nonstick cooking spray.

2. Spread oats on ungreased baking sheet. Bake 10 minutes or until fragrant and lightly browned, stirring occasionally. Pour into medium bowl; let cool slightly.

3. Whisk milk, pumpkin, eggs, brown sugar and vanilla in large bowl until well blended. Add ½ cup cranberries, pumpkin pie spice, salt and baking powder to oats; mix well. Add oat mixture to pumpkin mixture; stir until well blended. Pour into prepared baking dish.

4. Bake 45 minutes or until set and knife inserted into center comes out almost clean. Serve warm with maple syrup, additional cranberries and pecans, if desired.

SAUSAGE, EGG & CHILE CASSEROLE

MAKES 8 SERVINGS

- **1 pound bulk pork sausage**
- **2 stalks celery, chopped (about 1 cup)**
- **1 small onion, chopped (about ¼ cup)**
- **1 small green pepper, chopped (about ½ cup)**
- **1 small red pepper, chopped (about ½ cup)**
- **1 can (4 ounces) chopped green chiles, undrained**
- **8 slices PEPPERIDGE FARM® White Sandwich Bread, cut into cubes (about 4 cups)**
- **4 eggs**
- **3 cups milk**
- **1 can (10¾ ounces) CAMPBELL'S® Condensed Cream of Mushroom Soup (Regular OR 98% Fat Free)**
- **3 cups shredded mild Cheddar cheese (about 12 ounces)**

1. Cook the sausage in a 10-inch skillet over medium-high heat until well browned, stirring often to separate the meat. Pour off any fat.

2. Stir the celery, onion and peppers in the skillet and cook until tender, stirring occasionally. Stir in the chiles. Remove the skillet from the heat.

3. Place **HALF** the bread cubes into a lightly greased 3-quart shallow baking dish. Layer with the sausage mixture and remaining bread cubes. Beat the eggs and milk in a medium bowl with a fork or whisk. Pour the milk mixture over the bread cubes.

4. Bake at 350°F. for 45 minutes. Spoon the soup over the casserole. Sprinkle with the cheese.

5. Bake for 15 minutes or until the cheese is melted.

ROASTED PEPPER AND SOURDOUGH EGG DISH

MAKES 6 SERVINGS

3 cups sourdough bread cubes

1 jar (12 ounces) roasted red pepper strips, drained

1 cup (4 ounces) shredded Monterey Jack cheese

1 cup (4 ounces) shredded sharp Cheddar cheese

1 cup cottage cheese

6 eggs

1 cup milk

1/4 cup chopped fresh cilantro

1/4 teaspoon black pepper

SLOW COOKER DIRECTIONS

1. Coat inside of slow cooker with nonstick cooking spray. Add bread. Arrange roasted peppers evenly over bread cubes; sprinkle with Monterey Jack and Cheddar cheeses.

2. Place cottage cheese in food processor or blender; process until smooth. Add eggs and milk; process just until blended. Stir in cilantro and black pepper.

3. Pour egg mixture into slow cooker. Cover; cook on LOW 3 to 3½ hours or on HIGH 2 to 2½ hours or until eggs are firm but still moist.

CINNAMON WALNUT COFFEE CAKE

MAKES 12 TO 16 SERVINGS

³/₄ cup chopped walnuts

1 teaspoon ground cinnamon

1¼ cups sugar

1 cup (2 sticks) butter, softened

2 eggs

1 cup sour cream

1⅓ cups all-purpose flour

⅓ cup CREAM OF WHEAT® Cinnamon Swirl Instant Hot Cereal, uncooked

1½ teaspoons baking powder

½ teaspoon baking soda

1 teaspoon vanilla extract

1. Coat Bundt® pan with nonstick cooking spray. Sprinkle lightly with flour; shake out any excess. Combine walnuts and cinnamon in small bowl; set aside.

2. Cream sugar, butter and eggs in mixing bowl with electric mixer at medium speed. Add sour cream; blend well. Add flour, Cream of Wheat, baking powder and baking soda; mix well. Stir in vanilla. Sprinkle half of walnut mixture into bottom of prepared Bundt pan. Evenly spread half of batter over mixture. Sprinkle remaining walnut mixture over batter. Top with remaining batter, spreading evenly in Bundt pan.

3. Set oven to 350°F (do not preheat); place Bundt pan in cold oven. Bake 45 minutes or until toothpick inserted into center comes out clean. Remove from oven; let stand 5 minutes. Place serving plate over Bundt pan and turn pan over carefully onto plate; remove pan. Serve cake warm or cool.

TIP
If you do not have a Bundt®
pan, you can bake this cake
in regular square or round
cake pans. Divide the batter
between two 8- or 9-inch
pans, and sprinkle each with
one-half of walnut mixture.
Bake 25 to 30 minutes.

CRUSTLESS HAM & SPINACH TART

MAKES 4 SERVINGS

1 teaspoon olive oil

1 cup finely chopped onion

2 cloves garlic, minced

1 package (10 ounces) frozen chopped spinach, thawed and squeezed dry

3 slices deli ham, cut into strips (3 ounces total)

1 cup milk

3 eggs

¼ cup plus 2 tablespoons grated Parmesan cheese, divided

1 tablespoon minced fresh basil *or* 2 teaspoons dried basil

½ teaspoon black pepper

⅛ teaspoon ground nutmeg

1. Preheat oven to 350°F. Lightly spray 9-inch glass pie plate with nonstick cooking spray.

2. Heat oil in medium skillet over medium-high heat. Add onion; cook 2 minutes or until soft, stirring occasionally. Add garlic; cook 1 minute. Stir in spinach and ham. Spread mixture evenly in prepared pie plate.

3. Combine milk, eggs, ¼ cup cheese, basil, pepper and nutmeg in medium bowl; whisk to blend. Pour mixture over spinach mixture. Bake 50 minutes or until knife inserted into center comes out clean. Sprinkle with remaining 2 tablespoons cheese.

CHOCOLATE CHERRY PANCAKES

MAKES 20 TO 24 PANCAKES (6 TO 8 SERVINGS)

2 **cups all-purpose flour**

1 **cup dried cherries**

2/3 **cup semisweet chocolate chips**

1/3 **cup sugar**

4 1/2 **teaspoons baking powder**

1/2 **teaspoon baking soda**

1/2 **teaspoon salt**

1 1/2 **cups milk**

2 **eggs**

1/4 **cup (1/2 stick) butter, melted**

1. Combine flour, dried cherries, chocolate chips, sugar, baking powder, baking soda and salt in large bowl; mix well. Beat milk, eggs and butter in medium bowl until well blended.

2. Add milk mixture to flour mixture; stir just until moistened. (Add 1/4 to 1/2 cup additional milk if thinner pancakes are desired.)

3. Heat griddle or large nonstick skillet over medium heat until drop of water sizzles when dropped on surface. Pour batter onto griddle, 1/4 cup at a time. Cook 2 to 3 minutes on each side or until golden.

BERRY BUCKWHEAT SCONES

MAKES 8 SCONES

1¼ cups all-purpose flour

¾ cup buckwheat flour, plus additional for dusting

¼ cup packed brown sugar

1 tablespoon baking powder

½ teaspoon salt

½ cup (1 stick) cold unsalted butter, cubed

¾ cup fresh raspberries

¾ cup fresh blackberries

1 egg

½ cup whipping cream

1 tablespoon granulated sugar

Lemon curd or jam (optional)

1. Preheat oven to 375°F. Line baking sheet with parchment paper.

2. Combine all-purpose flour, ¾ cup buckwheat flour, brown sugar, baking powder and salt in bowl of food processor; pulse until combined. Add butter; pulse until pea-sized pieces of butter remain. Transfer mixture to large bowl; stir in berries.

3. Whisk egg and cream in small bowl. Stir cream mixture into flour mixture until soft dough forms.

4. Transfer dough to work surface lightly dusted with buckwheat flour; gently pat into an 8-inch round about ¾ inch thick. Cut into eight wedges.

5. Place wedges 1½ inches apart on prepared baking sheet. Sprinkle tops with granulated sugar. Bake 20 to 25 minutes or until golden. Remove to wire rack; cool 10 minutes.

6. Serve warm with jam or lemon curd, if desired.

PINEAPPLE CARROT RAISIN MUFFINS

MAKES 3 DOZEN MINI-MUFFINS

2 cups all-purpose flour

1 cup sugar

1½ teaspoons baking powder

1 teaspoon ground cinnamon

1 can (8 oz.) DOLE® Crushed Pineapple, undrained

2 eggs

½ cup (1 stick) butter or margarine, melted

1 cup DOLE® Seedless or Golden Raisins

½ cup shredded DOLE® Carrots

COMBINE flour, sugar, baking powder and cinnamon in large bowl.

ADD undrained pineapple, eggs, butter, raisins and carrots; stir just until blended.

SPOON evenly into 36 mini-muffin cups sprayed with nonstick vegetable cooking spray.

BAKE at 375°F., 15 to 20 minutes or until toothpick inserted in center comes out clean. Remove muffins from pans onto wire rack to cool.

For 2½-inch muffins: Spoon batter into 2½-inch muffin pans instead of mini-muffin pans. Bake as directed for 20 to 25 minutes. Cool as directed.

CHEESY QUICHETTES

MAKES 12 QUICHETTES

12 **slices bacon, crisp-cooked and chopped**

6 **eggs, beaten**

¼ **cup whole milk**

1½ **cups thawed frozen shredded hash brown potatoes, squeezed dry**

¼ **cup chopped fresh parsley**

½ **teaspoon salt**

1½ **cups (6 ounces) shredded Mexican cheese blend with jalapeño peppers**

1. Preheat oven to 400°F. Lightly spray 12 standard (2½-inch) muffin cups with nonstick cooking spray.

2. Divide bacon evenly among prepared muffin cups. Beat eggs and milk in medium bowl. Add potatoes, parsley and salt; mix well. Spoon mixture evenly into muffin cups.

3. Bake 15 minutes or until knife inserted into centers comes out almost clean. Sprinkle evenly with cheese; let stand 3 minutes or until cheese is melted. (Egg mixture will continue to cook while standing.) Gently run knife around edges and lift out with fork.

BAKED PUMPKIN FRENCH TOAST

MAKES 6 SERVINGS

1 tablespoon butter, softened

1 loaf challah or egg bread (12 to 16 ounces), cut into ¾-inch-thick slices

7 eggs

1¼ cups whole milk

⅔ cup canned pumpkin

1 teaspoon vanilla

½ teaspoon pumpkin pie spice

⅛ teaspoon salt

3 tablespoons sugar

2 teaspoons ground cinnamon

Maple syrup

1. Generously grease 13×9-inch baking dish with butter. Arrange bread slices in dish, fitting slices in tightly.

2. Combine eggs, milk, pumpkin, vanilla, pumpkin pie spice and salt in medium bowl; beat until well blended. Pour over bread in prepared baking dish; turn slices to coat completely. Cover; refrigerate 8 hours or overnight.

3. Preheat oven to 350°F. Combine sugar and cinnamon in small bowl; mix well. Turn bread slices again; sprinkle generously with cinnamon-sugar.

4. Bake 30 minutes or until bread is puffy and golden brown. Serve immediately with maple syrup.

JILL'S HASH BROWN CASSEROLE

MAKES 8 SERVINGS

- **1 can (10½ ounces) CAMPBELL'S® Condensed Cream of Mushroom Soup (Regular OR 98% Fat Free)**
- **1 container (8 ounces) sour cream**
- **½ cup butter, melted (1 stick)**
- **1 bag (32 ounces) frozen hash brown potatoes (about 7½ cups)**
- **1 medium onion, chopped (about ½ cup)**
- **1 package (8 ounces) shredded Cheddar cheese (2 cups)**
- **Ground black pepper**
- **½ cup crushed corn flakes**

1. Stir the soup, sour cream, butter, potatoes, onion and cheese in a 3-quart shallow baking dish. Season with the black pepper. Sprinkle the potato mixture evenly with the crushed corn flakes.

2. Bake at 350°F. for 45 minutes or until hot and bubbling.

BREAKFAST HASH

MAKES 6 TO 8 SERVINGS

1 **pound BOB EVANS® Special Seasonings or Savory Sage Roll Sausage**

2 **cups chopped potatoes**

¼ **cup chopped red and/or green bell pepper**

2 **tablespoons chopped onion**

6 **eggs**

2 **tablespoons milk**

Crumble sausage into large skillet. Add potatoes, pepper and onion. Cook over low heat until sausage is browned and potatoes are fork-tender, stirring occasionally. Drain off any drippings. Whisk eggs and milk in small bowl until blended. Add to sausage mixture; scramble until eggs are set but not dry. Serve hot. Refrigerate leftovers.

Serving Suggestion: Serve with fresh fruit.

RICH AND GOOEY CINNAMON BUNS

MAKES 12 BUNS

DOUGH

- **1 package (¼ ounce) active dry yeast**
- **1 cup warm milk (110°F)**
- **2 eggs, beaten**
- **½ cup granulated sugar**
- **¼ cup (½ stick) butter, softened**
- **1 teaspoon salt**
- **4 to 4¼ cups all-purpose flour**

FILLING

- **1 cup packed brown sugar**
- **3 tablespoons ground cinnamon**
- **Pinch of salt**
- **6 tablespoons (¾ stick) butter, softened**

ICING

- **1½ cups powdered sugar**
- **3 ounces cream cheese, softened**
- **¼ cup (½ stick) butter, softened**
- **½ teaspoon vanilla**
- **⅛ teaspoon salt**

1. Dissolve yeast in warm milk in large bowl of electric mixer. Add eggs, granulated sugar, ¼ cup butter and 1 teaspoon salt; beat at medium speed until well blended. Add 4 cups flour; beat at low speed until dough begins to come together. Knead dough with dough hook at low speed about 5 minutes or until smooth, elastic and slightly sticky. Add additional flour, 1 tablespoon at a time, if necessary to prevent sticking.

2. Shape dough into a ball. Place in large greased bowl; turn to grease top. Cover; let rise in warm place about 1 hour or until doubled in size. Meanwhile, for filling, combine brown sugar, cinnamon and pinch of salt in small bowl; mix well.

3. Spray 13×9-inch baking pan with nonstick cooking spray. Roll out dough into 18×14-inch rectangle on floured surface. Spread 6 tablespoons butter evenly over dough; top with cinnamon-sugar mixture. Beginning with long side, roll up dough tightly jelly-roll style; pinch seam to seal. Cut log crosswise into 12 slices; place slices cut sides up in prepared pan. Cover; let rise in warm place about 30 minutes or until almost doubled in size. Preheat oven to 350°F.

4. Bake 20 to 25 minutes or until golden brown. Meanwhile, for icing, combine powdered sugar, cream cheese, ¼ cup butter, vanilla and ⅛ teaspoon salt in medium bowl; beat with electric mixer at medium speed 2 minutes or until smooth and creamy. Spread icing generously over warm cinnamon buns.

DENVER BRUNCH BAKE

MAKES 4 SERVINGS

|||||||||||||||||||||||||||||||||||||||||||||||||||||||||||||||||||||||||||||||||||||||||||||||||||||||||||||||||||||||||||||||||||||||||||||||||

  2 **tablespoons butter, divided**

½ **cup diced onion**

½ **cup diced green bell pepper**

½ **cup diced red bell pepper**

½ **cup cubed ham**

  6 **eggs**

  1 **cup whole milk**

½ **teaspoon salt**

¼ **teaspoon red pepper flakes**

  4 **slices white sandwich bread, cut into ½-inch cubes**

¾ **cup (3 ounces) shredded Cheddar cheese, divided**

1. Grease 9-inch baking dish with 1 tablespoon butter.

2. Melt remaining 1 tablespoon butter in large skillet over medium heat. Add onion and bell peppers; cook and stir 3 minutes. Add ham; cook and stir 2 minutes.

3. Beat eggs, milk, salt and red pepper flakes in large bowl. Add bread cubes, ham mixture and ½ cup cheese; mix well. Pour into prepared dish. Cover; refrigerate 8 hours or overnight.

4. Preheat oven to 350°F. Sprinkle casserole with remaining ¼ cup cheese.

5. Bake 45 minutes to 1 hour or until knife inserted into center comes out clean.

CHEESE BLINTZES

MAKES ABOUT 14 BLINTZES

- 1 **cup rice flour**
- ¼ **teaspoon salt**
- ¼ **teaspoon ground nutmeg**
- 1 **cup half-and-half**
- 3 **tablespoons butter, melted, divided**
- 1½ **teaspoons vanilla, divided**
- 3 **eggs**
- 1 **container (15 ounces) ricotta cheese**
- 2 **tablespoons powdered sugar**

  Cherry pie filling, preserves, applesauce or sour cream

1. Combine rice flour, salt and nutmeg in medium bowl. Gradually whisk in half-and-half until smooth.

2. Add 2 tablespoons butter and ½ teaspoon vanilla. Whisk in eggs, one at a time, until batter is smooth with the consistency of heavy cream.

3. Heat 8- or 9-inch nonstick skillet over medium heat. Brush lightly with some of remaining butter. Pour about ¼ cup batter into center of pan. Immediately swirl pan to coat with batter. Cook about 1 minute or until crêpe is dull on top and edges are dry. Turn and cook 30 seconds. Remove to plate; keep warm. Repeat with remaining batter.

4. Meanwhile, combine ricotta, powdered sugar and remaining 1 teaspoon vanilla in medium bowl. Fill crêpes with ricotta mixture. Serve with cherry pie filling.

BACON CHEDDAR MONKEY BREAD

MAKES 12 SERVINGS

1¾ cups (7 ounces) shredded sharp Cheddar cheese

12 ounces bacon, cooked and chopped (about 1 cup)

¼ cup finely chopped green onions

2¾ to 3 cups all-purpose flour, divided

1 package (¼ ounce) rapid-rise active dry yeast

1 teaspoon salt

1 cup warm water (120°F)

2 tablespoons olive oil

⅓ cup butter, melted

1 egg

1. Combine cheese, bacon and green onions in medium bowl; mix well.

2. Combine 1½ cups flour, yeast and salt in large bowl of electric stand mixer; stir to combine. Add water and oil; beat at medium speed 3 minutes.

3. Replace paddle attachment with dough hook; beat in 1¼ cups flour until dough comes together. Add 1 cup cheese mixture; knead at medium-low speed 6 to 8 minutes or until dough is smooth and elastic, adding remaining ¼ cup flour if necessary to clean side of bowl. Place dough in greased bowl; turn to grease top. Cover; let rise in warm place 30 minutes or until doubled in size.

4. Generously spray 12-cup (10-inch) bundt pan with nonstick cooking spray. Whisk butter and egg in shallow bowl until blended. Punch down dough. Roll 1-inch pieces of dough into balls. Dip balls in butter mixture; roll in remaining cheese mixture to coat. Layer in prepared pan. Cover; let rise in warm place 40 minutes or until almost doubled in size. Preheat oven to 375°F.

5. Bake 35 minutes or until golden brown. Loosen edges of bread with knife; invert onto wire rack. Cool 5 minutes; serve warm.

APPETIZER PARTY

CHEESY GARLIC BREAD

MAKES 8 TO 10 SERVINGS

1 loaf (about 16 ounces) Italian bread

$1/2$ cup (1 stick) butter, softened

8 cloves garlic, very thinly sliced

$1/4$ cup grated Parmesan cheese

2 cups (8 ounces) shredded mozzarella cheese

1. Preheat oven to 425°F. Line large baking sheet with foil.

2. Cut bread in half horizontally. Spread cut sides of bread evenly with butter; top with sliced garlic. Sprinkle with Parmesan, then mozzarella cheeses. Place on prepared baking sheet.

3. Bake 12 minutes or until cheeses are melted and golden brown in spots. Cut crosswise into slices. Serve warm.

SAUCY TACO FRANKS

MAKES 4 TO 6 SERVINGS

1 jar (8 ounces) ORTEGA®
Taco Sauce, Medium

1 jar (12 ounces) POLANER®
ALL FRUIT® Grape Fruit
Spread

1 package (16 ounces) cocktail
franks

1 packet (1.25 ounces)
ORTEGA® Taco Seasoning
Mix

Combine taco sauce and fruit spread in medium skillet. Add cocktail franks. Mix well to coat franks.

Heat over medium heat. Cook and stir until fruit spread melts and mixture begins to bubble. Stir in seasoning mix; reduce heat. Simmer 5 minutes or until sauce thickens and franks are thoroughly heated. Serve warm.

VARIATION: Try using ORTEGA®'s Chipotle Taco Seasoning Mix for a smokier flavor.

TIP

You can use your slow cooker to keep these tasty appetizers warm throughout your party. Just keep the setting on "low" or "warm" and keep the lid on.

MINI TWICE BAKED POTATOES WITH SPICED RAMEN CRISPIES

MAKES 24 PIECES

‖‖

- 2 **pounds small new potatoes, about 1½ to 2 inches in diameter**
- 1 **package (8 ounces) cream cheese, softened**
- 1 **cup sour cream**
- 1 **cup cooked crumbled bacon, divided**
- ½ **teaspoon garlic powder**
- 1 **teaspoon salt, divided**
- ½ **teaspoon black pepper**
- ½ **cup (2 ounces) finely shredded sharp Cheddar cheese**
- ¼ **cup finely chopped green onions, plus additional for garnish**
- 1 **package (3 ounces) ramen noodles, any flavor, crumbled***
- 1 **teaspoon chili powder**
- ½ **teaspoon ground cumin**

*Discard seasoning packet.

1. Preheat oven to 400°F. Line large baking sheet with foil.

2. Combine potatoes and enough water to cover in Dutch oven; season with salt. Bring to a boil; boil until just tender, about 10 to 12 minutes. Drain and rinse with cold water to cool quickly, shaking off excess liquid.

3. Cut potatoes in half crosswise. Cut thin slice off round end of each potato half to stand upright. Using melon baller or small spoon, scoop out centers of potatoes, leaving ¼-inch thick shell. Place "meat" of potato in medium bowl. Add cream cheese, sour cream, ½ cup bacon, garlic powder, ½ teaspoon salt and pepper. Mash with potato masher until well combined. Stir in Cheddar cheese and ¼ cup green onions.

4. Sprinkle insides of potato shells with remaining ½ teaspoon salt. Spoon potato mixture evenly into shells.

5. Stir noodles, remaining bacon, chili powder and cumin in medium bowl. Sprinkle evenly over potatoes. Bake 15 to 20 minutes or until lightly browned. Serve sprinkled with additional green onions, if desired.

DILLY DEVILED EGGS

MAKES 6 SERVINGS

6 **hard-cooked eggs, peeled and sliced in half lengthwise**

1 **tablespoon sour cream**

1 **tablespoon mayonnaise**

1 **tablespoon cottage cheese**

1 **tablespoon minced fresh dill** *or* **1 teaspoon dried dill weed**

1 **tablespoon minced dill pickle**

1 **teaspoon Dijon mustard**

⅛ **teaspoon salt**

⅛ **teaspoon white pepper**

Paprika (optional)

Fresh dill sprigs (optional)

1. Remove yolks from egg halves. Mash yolks with sour cream, mayonnaise, cottage cheese, dill, pickle, mustard, salt and pepper in small bowl.

2. Fill egg halves with yolk mixture using teaspoon or piping bag fitted with large plain tip. Garnish filled egg halves with paprika and dill sprigs.

BAKED APRICOT BRIE

MAKES 6 SERVINGS

1 **round (8 ounces) Brie cheese**

⅓ **cup apricot preserves**

2 **tablespoons sliced almonds**

Cracked pepper or other assorted crackers

1. Preheat oven to 400°F. Place cheese in small baking pan. Spread top of cheese with preserves; sprinkle with almonds.

2. Bake 10 to 12 minutes or until cheese begins to melt and lose its shape. Serve hot with crackers. Refrigerate any leftovers.

NOTE: Brie is a soft-ripened, unpressed cheese made from cow's milk. It has a distinctive round shape, edible white rind and creamy yellow interior. Avoid Brie that has a chalky center (it is underripe) or a strong ammonia odor (it is overripe). The cheese should give slightly to pressure and have an evenly colored, barely moist rind.

CHICKEN FAJITA NACHOS

MAKES 4 SERVINGS

- 2 **tablespoons vegetable oil, divided**
- 2 **red bell peppers, cut into thin strips**
- 1 **large onion, halved and thinly sliced**
- 2 **tablespoons fajita seasoning mix (from 1¼-ounce package), divided**
- 2 **tablespoons water, divided**
- 1 **large boneless skinless chicken breast (about 12 ounces), cut into 2×1-inch strips**
- 4 **cups tortilla chips (about 30 chips)**
- ½ **cup (2 ounces) shredded Cheddar cheese**
- ½ **cup (2 ounces) shredded Monterey Jack cheese**
- 1 **jalapeño pepper,* seeded and thinly sliced**
- 1 **cup shredded lettuce**
- ½ **cup salsa**
  Sour cream and guacamole (optional)

*Jalapeño peppers can sting and irritate the skin, so wear rubber gloves when handling peppers and do not touch your eyes.

1. Heat 1 tablespoon oil in large skillet over medium-high heat. Add bell peppers and onion; cook 5 minutes or until tender and browned in spots, stirring frequently. Transfer to large bowl; stir in 1 tablespoon fajita seasoning mix and 1 tablespoon water.

2. Heat remaining 1 tablespoon oil in same skillet over medium-high heat. Add chicken; cook 7 to 10 minutes, stirring occasionally. Add remaining 1 tablespoon fajita seasoning mix and 1 tablespoon water; cook and stir 3 to 5 minutes or until chicken is coated.

3. Preheat broiler. Place chips in 11×7-inch baking dish or pan; top with vegetables, chicken, Cheddar and Monterey Jack cheeses and jalapeño.

4. Broil 2 to 4 minutes or until cheeses are melted. Top with lettuce, salsa, sour cream and guacamole, if desired.

ELEGANT APPETIZER BITES

MAKES 30 APPETIZERS

1 **package (8 ounces) cream cheese, softened**

2 **ounces feta cheese with basil and tomato or plain feta cheese**

2 **cloves garlic, minced**

30 **mini phyllo shells (two 2.1-ounce packages) *or* 15 mini puff pastry shells**

Prepared toppings such as sundried tomato pesto, red pepper and artichoke tapenade, basil pesto and/ or black olive spread

1. Beat cream cheese, feta cheese and garlic in small bowl with electric mixer at low speed until well combined.

2. Spoon about 1½ teaspoons cheese mixture into each shell. Top with ½ teaspoon desired topping. Serve immediately or cover and refrigerate until ready to serve.

CHICKEN TORTILLA ROLL-UPS

MAKES ABOUT 18 SLICES

- **4 ounces cream cheese, softened**
- **2 tablespoons mayonnaise**
- **1 tablespoon Dijon mustard**
- **1/4 teaspoon black pepper**
- **3 (10- or 12-inch) flour tortillas**
- **1 cup finely chopped cooked chicken**
- **3/4 cup shredded or finely chopped carrot**
- **3/4 cup finely chopped green bell pepper**
- **3 tablespoons chopped green onions**

1. Combine cream cheese, mayonnaise, mustard and black pepper in small bowl; stir until well blended.

2. Spread cream cheese mixture evenly onto each tortilla leaving ½-inch border. Sprinkle chicken, carrot, bell pepper and green onions evenly over cream cheese leaving 1½-inch border on cream cheese mixture at one end of each tortilla.

3. Roll up each tortilla jelly-roll fashion. Cut rolls into 1½-inch-thick slices.

COOK'S NOOK: Wrap rolls in plastic wrap and refrigerate for several hours for easier slicing and to allow flavors to blend.

CRAB-STUFFED TOMATOES

MAKES 8 TO 10 SERVINGS

16 large cherry tomatoes (1½ inches in diameter)

3 tablespoons mayonnaise

½ teaspoon lemon juice

1 small clove garlic, minced

¾ cup fresh or refrigerated canned crabmeat*

3 tablespoons chopped pimiento-stuffed green olives

2 tablespoons slivered almonds or pinenuts

⅛ teaspoon black pepper

Choose special grade crabmeat for this recipe. It is less expensive and already flaked but just as flavorful as backfin, lump or claw meat. Look for it in the refrigerated seafood section of the supermarket. Shelf-stable canned crabmeat can be substituted.

1. Cut small slivers from bottoms of cherry tomatoes so they will stand upright. Cut off top of tomatoes; scoop out seeds and membranes. Turn tomatoes upside down to drain; set aside.

2. Combine mayonnaise, lemon juice and garlic in medium bowl. Add crabmeat, olives, almonds and pepper; stir gently to coat.

3. Spoon crab mixture into tomatoes. Serve immediately.

NOTE: If large cherry tomatoes are unavailable, you can substitute 4 small plum tomatoes. Cut tomatoes in half lengthwise; scoop out seeds and membranes. Turn cut sides down to drain; set aside. Proceed as directed above.

TIP

For the best flavor, do not refrigerate the stuffed tomatoes. Crab mixture can be prepared several hours in advance and refrigerated. Stuff tomatoes with the crab mixture just before serving. Or the crab mixture can be served on crackers or toasted French bread rounds.

BUFFALO WINGS

MAKES 4 SERVINGS

|||||||||||||||||||||||||||||||||||||||||||||||||||||||||||||||||||||||||||||||||||||||||||||||||||||||||||||||||||||||||||||||||

1 **cup hot pepper sauce**

⅓ **cup vegetable oil, plus additional for frying**

1 **teaspoon sugar**

½ **teaspoon ground red pepper**

½ **teaspoon garlic powder**

½ **teaspoon Worcestershire sauce**

⅛ **teaspoon black pepper**

1 **pound chicken wings, tips discarded, separated at joints**

Blue cheese or ranch dressing

Celery sticks

1. Combine hot pepper sauce, ⅓ cup oil, sugar, red pepper, garlic powder, Worcestershire sauce and black pepper in small saucepan; cook over medium heat 20 minutes. Remove from heat; pour sauce into large bowl.

2. Heat 3 inches of oil in large saucepan over medium-high heat to 350°F; adjust heat to maintain temperature. Add wings; cook 10 minutes or until crispy. Drain on wire rack set over paper towels.

3. Transfer wings to bowl of sauce; toss to coat. Serve with blue cheese dressing and celery sticks.

MAPLE-GLAZED MEATBALLS

MAKES ABOUT 48 MEATBALLS

- 2 packages (about 16 ounces each) frozen fully cooked meatballs, partially thawed and separated
- 1 can (20 ounces) pineapple chunks in juice, drained
- 1½ cups ketchup
- 1 cup maple syrup
- ⅓ cup soy sauce
- 1 tablespoon quick-cooking tapioca
- 1 teaspoon dry mustard
- ½ teaspoon ground allspice

SLOW COOKER DIRECTIONS

1. Combine meatballs, pineapple chunks, ketchup, maple syrup, soy sauce, tapioca, mustard and allspice in slow cooker; mix well.

2. Cover; cook on LOW 5 to 6 hours. Stir before serving.

COCKTAIL SHRIMP

MAKES 6 SERVINGS

1 pound medium raw shrimp, peeled and deveined

¼ teaspoon salt

¼ teaspoon black pepper

¼ teaspoon ground red pepper, divided (optional)

½ cup ketchup

1 to 2 tablespoons prepared horseradish

1½ teaspoons lemon juice

1 teaspoon Worcestershire sauce

⅛ teaspoon hot pepper sauce

Lemon wedges (optional)

1. Heat large nonstick skillet over medium heat; spray with nonstick cooking spray. Add shrimp; season with salt, black pepper and ⅛ teaspoon red pepper, if desired. Cook and stir 5 to 6 minutes or until shrimp are pink and opaque. Remove from heat; drain well. Cool completely.

2. Stir ketchup, horseradish, lemon juice, Worcestershire sauce, remaining ⅛ teaspoon red pepper, if desired, and hot pepper sauce in small bowl until well blended.

3. Serve shrimp with cocktail sauce and lemon wedges, if desired.

ARUGULA-PROSCIUTTO WRAPPED BREADSTICKS WITH GARLIC MUSTARD SAUCE

MAKES 16 APPETIZERS

½ **cup mayonnaise**

6 **tablespoons grated Parmesan cheese**

2 **tablespoons FRENCH'S® Honey Dijon Mustard**

1 **tablespoon chopped fresh basil**

2 **teaspoons minced garlic**

1 **package (4½ ounces) long breadsticks (12 to 16 breadsticks)**

1⅓ **cups FRENCH'S® French Fried Onions, crushed**

½ **pound thinly sliced prosciutto or smoked deli ham**

1 **bunch arugula (about 20 leaves) or green leaf lettuce, washed, drained and stems removed**

1. Combine mayonnaise, cheese, mustard, basil and garlic in mixing bowl. Spread half of each breadstick with some of mustard sauce. Roll in French Fried Onions, pressing firmly.

2. Arrange prosciutto slices on flat work surface. Top each slice with leaf of arugula. Place coated end of breadsticks on top; roll up jelly-roll style. Place seam side down on serving platter.

3. Serve wrapped breadsticks with remaining mustard sauce for dipping.

ANTIPASTO WITH MARINATED MUSHROOMS

MAKES 6 TO 8 SERVINGS

Marinated Mushrooms
(recipe follows)

4 teaspoons red wine vinegar

½ teaspoon dried basil

½ teaspoon dried oregano

⅛ teaspoon black pepper

¼ cup extra virgin olive oil

4 ounces mozzarella cheese,
cut into ½-inch cubes

4 ounces prosciutto or cooked
ham, thinly sliced

4 ounces provolone cheese,
cut into 2-inch sticks

1 jar (10 ounces) pepperoncini
peppers, drained

8 ounces hard salami, thinly
sliced

2 jars (6 ounces each)
marinated artichoke
hearts, drained

6 ounces black olives

Fresh basil leaves or chives
(optional)

1. Prepare Marinated Mushrooms; set aside. Combine vinegar, dried basil, oregano and black pepper in small bowl. Add oil; whisk until well blended. Add mozzarella cubes; stir to coat. Marinate, covered, in refrigerator at least 2 hours.

2. Drain mozzarella cubes, reserving marinade. Wrap 1 prosciutto slice around each provolone stick.

3. Arrange mozzarella cubes, prosciutto-wrapped provolone sticks, Marinated Mushrooms, pepperoncini, salami, artichoke hearts and olives on large platter. Drizzle reserved marinade over artichoke hearts and olives. Garnish with fresh basil. Serve with small forks or toothpicks.

MARINATED MUSHROOMS | MAKES ½ POUND

- **3 tablespoons lemon juice**
- **2 tablespoons chopped fresh parsley**
- **1 clove garlic, crushed**
- **½ teaspoon salt**
- **¼ teaspoon dried tarragon**
- **⅛ teaspoon black pepper**
- **½ cup extra virgin olive oil**
- **½ pound small or medium fresh mushrooms, stems removed**

1. Combine lemon juice, parsley, garlic, salt, tarragon and pepper in medium bowl. Add oil; whisk until well blended. Add mushrooms; stir to coat. Marinate, covered, in refrigerator 4 hours or overnight, stirring occasionally.

2. Drain mushrooms; reserve marinade for dressing.

CALIFORNIA HAM ROLLS

MAKES 4 SERVINGS

2 **cups water**

½ **teaspoon salt, divided**

1 **cup uncooked short grain brown rice**

2 **tablespoons unseasoned rice vinegar* or cider vinegar**

1 **tablespoon sugar**

4 **(8-inch) sheets sushi nori***

8 **thin strips ham (about 4 ounces)**

¼ **cup soy sauce**

1 **tablespoon mirin (sweet rice wine)***

1 **tablespoon minced fresh chives**

*These ingredients may be found in the Asian section of your supermarket.

1. Bring water and ¼ teaspoon salt to a boil in medium saucepan over high heat. Stir in rice. Reduce heat to low. Cover; simmer 40 to 45 minutes or until water is absorbed and rice is tender but chewy. Spoon rice into large shallow bowl.

2. Combine vinegar, sugar and remaining ¼ teaspoon salt in small bowl. Microwave on HIGH 30 seconds. Stir to dissolve sugar. Pour over rice; stir to mix well. Set aside to cool.

3. Place 1 sheet of nori on work surface. Loosely spread about ½ cup rice over nori, leaving ½-inch border. Place 2 strips of ham along width of nori. Moisten top edge of nori sheet. Roll up tightly. Gently press to redistribute rice, if necessary. Cut into six slices with sharp knife. Place cut side up on serving plate. Repeat with remaining nori, rice and ham.

4. Combine soy sauce and mirin in small bowl. Sprinkle with chives. Serve with ham rolls.

CORN SALSA

MAKES 8 SERVINGS

- ½ **cup WISH-BONE® Italian Dressing**
- 1 **can (11 ounces) whole kernel corn, drained (about 1½ cups)**
- 1 **medium tomato, chopped (about 1 cup)**
- 1 **medium cucumber, peeled, seeded and chopped (about 1 cup)**
- ¼ **cup finely chopped red onion**
- 4 **teaspoons finely chopped jalapeño pepper, or hot pepper sauce to taste (optional)**
- 1 **tablespoon finely chopped fresh cilantro (optional)**
- 1 **teaspoon grated lime peel**

Combine all ingredients in medium bowl. Cover and marinate in refrigerator at least 30 minutes. Serve chilled or at room temperature with your favorite grilled foods.

BAKED SPINACH BALLS

MAKES 12 SERVINGS

- **2 cups sage and onion or herb-seasoned bread stuffing mix**
- **1 small onion, chopped**
- **2 tablespoons grated Parmesan cheese**
- **1 clove garlic, minced**
- **¼ teaspoon dried thyme**
- **¼ teaspoon black pepper**
- **1 package (10 ounces) frozen chopped spinach, thawed and well drained**
- **¼ cup chicken broth**
- **2 egg whites, beaten**
- **Dijon or honey mustard (optional)**

1. Combine bread stuffing mix, onion, cheese, garlic, thyme and pepper in medium bowl; mix well. Combine spinach, broth and egg whites in separate medium bowl; mix well. Stir into bread cube mixture. Cover; refrigerate 1 hour or until mixture is firm.

2. Preheat oven to 350°F. Shape mixture into 24 balls; place on ungreased baking sheet. Bake 15 minutes or until spinach balls are browned. Serve with mustard for dipping, if desired.

BACON, BLUE CHEESE & RAMEN BITES

MAKES 8 SERVINGS (ABOUT 24 PIECES)

2 packages (3 ounces each) ramen noodles, any flavor, broken into 1×2-inch pieces*

¼ teaspoon black pepper, preferably coarsely ground

¼ cup roasted red peppers, chopped and patted dry on paper towels

¾ to 1 cup crumbled blue cheese

4 slices thick-cut bacon, cooked and crumbled

2 medium green onions, green part only, chopped

*Discard seasoning packets.

1. Preheat oven to 400°F. Line 13×9-inch baking pan with foil. Spray with nonstick cooking spray.

2. Place noodle pieces on prepared baking pan; sprinkle with black pepper. Top with red peppers, blue cheese, bacon and green onions.

3. Bake, uncovered, 12 to 15 minutes or until cheese bubbles. Serve hot or at room temperature.

SERVING SUGGESTIONS: For a more pronounced flavor and more crunch, serve hot. For more blended flavor with a slight crunch, serve at room temperature.

CLASSIC GUACAMOLE

MAKES ABOUT 2 CUPS

|||||||||||||||||||||||||||||||||||||||||||||||||||||||||||||||||||||||||||||||||||||||||||||||||||||||||||||||||||||

Corn Tortilla Chips (recipe follows) or packaged corn tortilla chips

4 tablespoons finely chopped white onion, divided

1 to 2 serrano or jalapeño peppers,* seeded and finely chopped

1½ tablespoons coarsely chopped fresh cilantro, divided

¼ teaspoon chopped garlic (optional)

2 large ripe avocados

1 medium tomato, peeled and chopped

1 to 2 teaspoons fresh lime juice

¼ teaspoon salt

*Serrano and jalapeño peppers can sting and irritate the skin, so wear rubber gloves when handling peppers and do not touch your eyes.

1. Prepare Corn Tortilla Chips.

2. Combine 2 tablespoons onion, serrano pepper, 1 tablespoon cilantro and garlic, if desired, in large mortar. Grind with pestle until almost smooth. (Mixture can be processed in food processor, if necessary, but it may become more watery than desired.)

3. Cut avocados into halves; remove and discard pits. Scoop out pulp; place in large bowl. Add serrano mixture; mash roughly, leaving avocado slightly chunky.

4. Add tomato, lime juice, salt, remaining 2 tablespoons onion and ½ tablespoon cilantro to avocado mixture; mix well. Serve immediately with Corn Tortilla Chips or cover and refrigerate up to 4 hours.

TIP

The Corn Tortilla Chips can be served with salsa, used as the base for nachos and used as scoops for guacamole, refried beans or other dips. They are best eaten fresh, but can be stored, tightly covered, in a cool place 2 to 3 days. Reheat in 350°F oven a few minutes before serving.

CORN TORTILLA CHIPS | MAKES 6 DOZEN

12 **(6-inch) corn tortillas, day-old***

Vegetable oil

½ **to 1 teaspoon salt**

*If tortillas are fresh, let stand, uncovered, in single layer on wire rack 1 to 2 hours to dry slightly.

1. Stack 6 tortillas. Cutting through stack, cut into 6 equal wedges. Repeat with remaining tortillas.

2. Heat ½ inch oil in large heavy skillet over medium-high heat to 375°F; adjust heat to maintain temperature.

3. Fry tortilla wedges in single layer 1 minute or until crisp, turning occasionally. Remove and drain on paper towels. Sprinkle chips with salt. Repeat with remaining wedges.

SOUPS & SALADS

FARRO, CHICKPEA AND SPINACH SALAD

MAKES 4 TO 6 ENTRÉE SALADS (OR 8 TO 12 SIDE SALADS)

1 cup uncooked pearled farro

3 cups baby spinach, stemmed

1 medium cucumber, chopped

1 can (about 15 ounces) chickpeas, rinsed and drained

3/4 cup pitted kalamata olives

1/4 cup extra virgin olive oil

3 tablespoons white or golden balsamic vinegar *or* 3 tablespoons cider vinegar mixed with 1/2 teaspoon sugar

1 teaspoon chopped fresh rosemary

1 clove garlic, minced

1 teaspoon salt

1/8 to 1/4 teaspoon red pepper flakes (optional)

1/2 cup crumbled goat or feta cheese

1. Bring 4 cups water to a boil in medium saucepan. Add farro; reduce heat and simmer 20 to 25 minutes or until farro is tender. Drain and rinse under cold water until cool.

2. Meanwhile, combine spinach, cucumber, chickpeas, olives, oil, vinegar, rosemary, garlic, salt and red pepper flakes, if desired, in large bowl. Stir in farro until well blended. Add cheese; stir gently.

ROASTED SWEET POTATO SOUP

MAKES 8 SERVINGS

5 **medium sweet potatoes (about 2 pounds)**

2 **tablespoons butter**

1 **medium onion, chopped (about 1 cup)**

2 **stalks celery, chopped (about 1 cup)**

6 **cups SWANSON® Chicken Broth (Regular, Natural Goodness® OR Certified Organic)**

1 **medium potato, peeled and cut into cubes (about 1 cup)**

⅓ **cup maple syrup**

⅛ **teaspoon ground white pepper**

2 **tablespoons light cream (optional)**

1. Pierce the sweet potatoes with a fork. Microwave on HIGH for 8 to 13 minutes or bake at 400°F. for 1 hour or until fork-tender. Cut in half lengthwise. Scoop out sweet potato pulp and set aside.

2. Heat the butter in a 6-quart saucepot over medium heat. Add the onion and celery to the saucepot and cook until tender. Add the broth and potato. Heat to a boil. Reduce the heat to low. Cook for 15 minutes or until the potato is tender. Add the maple syrup, white pepper and reserved sweet potato.

3. Place ⅓ of the broth mixture into an electric blender or food processor container. Cover and blend until smooth. Pour the mixture into a large bowl. Repeat the blending process twice more with the remaining broth mixture. Return all of the puréed mixture to the saucepot. Add the cream, if desired. Cook over medium heat until the mixture is hot. Season to taste.

TIP
Substitute **3¾ CUPS** mashed, drained, canned sweet potatoes for the fresh sweet potatoes.

ITALIAN WEDDING SOUP

MAKES 8 SERVINGS

2 **eggs**

2 **cloves garlic, minced**

1 **teaspoon salt**

$1/8$ **teaspoon black pepper**

MEATBALLS

$1^1/_2$ **pounds meat loaf mix (ground beef and pork)**

$3/_4$ **cup plain dry bread crumbs**

$1/_2$ **cup grated Parmesan cheese**

SOUP

2 **tablespoons olive oil**

1 **onion, chopped**

2 **carrots, chopped**

4 **cloves garlic, minced**

2 **heads escarole or curly endive, coarsely chopped**

8 **cups chicken broth**

1 **can (about 14 ounces) Italian plum tomatoes, coarsely chopped, juice reserved**

3 **fresh thyme sprigs**

1 **teaspoon salt**

$1/_2$ **teaspoon red pepper flakes**

1 **cup uncooked acini di pepe pasta**

1. Whisk eggs, 2 cloves garlic, 1 teaspoon salt and black pepper in large bowl until blended. Stir in meat loaf mix, bread crumbs and cheese; mix gently until well blended. Shape mixture by tablespoonfuls into 1-inch balls.

2. Heat oil in large saucepan or Dutch oven over medium heat. Cook meatballs in batches 5 minutes or until browned. Remove to plate; set aside.

3. Add onion, carrots and 4 cloves garlic to saucepan; cook and stir 5 minutes or until onion is lightly browned. Add escarole; cook 2 minutes or until wilted. Stir in broth, tomatoes, thyme, 1 teaspoon salt and red pepper flakes; bring to a boil over high heat. Reduce heat to medium-low; cook 15 minutes.

4. Add meatballs and pasta to soup; return to a boil over high heat. Reduce heat to medium; cook 10 minutes or until pasta is tender. Remove thyme sprigs before serving.

HOUSE SALAD

MAKES 4 SERVINGS

||||||||||||||||||||||||||||||||||||||||||||||||||||||||||||||||||||||||||||||||||||||||||||||||||||||||||||||||||||||||

Homemade Croutons

DRESSING

- ½ **cup mayonnaise**
- ½ **cup white wine vinegar**
- ¼ **cup grated Parmesan cheese**
- 1 **tablespoon olive oil**
- 1 **tablespoon lemon juice**
- 1 **tablespoon corn syrup**
- 1 **clove garlic, minced**
- ¾ **teaspoon Italian seasoning**
- ½ **teaspoon salt**
- ½ **teaspoon black pepper**

SALAD

- 1 **package (10 ounces) Italian salad blend**
- 2 **plum tomatoes, thinly sliced**
- ½ **cup thinly sliced red or green bell pepper**
- ½ **cup thinly sliced red onion**
- ¼ **cup sliced black olives**
   Pepperoncini (optional)

1. Prepare Homemade Croutons.

2. For dressing, whisk mayonnaise, vinegar, cheese, oil, lemon juice, corn syrup, garlic, Italian seasoning, salt and black pepper in medium bowl until well blended.

3. For salad, place salad blend in large bowl; top with tomatoes, 1 cup Homemade Croutons, bell pepper, onion, olives and pepperoncini, if desired. Add dressing; toss to coat.

HOMEMADE CROUTONS: Preheat oven to 350°F. Cut any kind of bread into ½- to 1-inch cubes. Hearty bread like whole wheat, tuscan or sour dough work best but sandwich bread works too. Spread the bread on a sheet pan and drizzle with olive oil. Toss with a spatula or your hands to coat. The bread should be evenly coated so add more oil if needed and toss again. If you want, season with salt and black pepper and a dried herb like oregano, thyme or rosemary. Bake 10 to 15 minutes or until bread is golden brown, stirring once or twice. Cool on pan before using.

FRESH TOMATO PASTA SOUP

MAKES 8 SERVINGS

1 tablespoon olive oil

½ cup chopped onion

1 clove garlic, minced

3 pounds fresh tomatoes (about 9 medium), coarsely chopped

3 cups chicken broth

1 tablespoon minced fresh basil

1 tablespoon minced fresh marjoram

1 tablespoon minced fresh oregano

1 teaspoon whole fennel seeds

½ teaspoon black pepper

¾ cup uncooked rosamarina, orzo or other small pasta

½ cup (2 ounces) shredded part-skim mozzarella cheese

1. Heat oil in large saucepan over medium heat. Add onion and garlic; cook and stir until onion is tender.

2. Add tomatoes, broth, basil, marjoram, oregano, fennel seeds and pepper; bring to a boil. Reduce heat to low; cover and simmer 25 minutes. Remove from heat; cool slightly.

3. Purée tomato mixture in batches in food processor or blender. Return to saucepan; bring to a boil. Add pasta; cook 7 to 9 minutes or until tender. Sprinkle with cheese.

HEIRLOOM TOMATO QUINOA SALAD

MAKES 4 SERVINGS

- **1 cup uncooked quinoa**
- **2 cups water**
- **2 tablespoons olive oil**
- **1 tablespoon lemon juice**
- **1 clove garlic, minced**
- **1/2 teaspoon salt**
- **2 cups assorted heirloom grape tomatoes (red, yellow or a combination), halved**
- **1/4 cup crumbled feta cheese**
- **1/4 cup chopped fresh basil, plus additional basil leaves for garnish**

1. Place quinoa in fine-mesh strainer; rinse well under cold running water. Bring 2 cups water to a boil in small saucepan; stir in quinoa. Reduce heat to low; cover and simmer 10 to 15 minutes or until quinoa is tender and water is absorbed.

2. Meanwhile, whisk oil, lemon juice, garlic and salt in large bowl until well blended. Gently stir in tomatoes and quinoa. Cover; refrigerate at least 30 minutes.

3. Stir in cheese just before serving. Top each serving with 1 tablespoon chopped basil. Garnish with additional basil leaves.

TAKE A TACO SALAD

MAKES 4 (1-QUART) JARS

DRESSING

- ¼ **cup mayonnaise**
- ¼ **cup plain yogurt or sour cream**
- 1 **tablespoon lime juice**
- ½ **teaspoon chipotle chili powder**
- 1 **clove garlic, minced**
- ¼ **cup crumbled cotija cheese**
- ¼ **cup chopped fresh cilantro**

SALAD

- 1 **tablespoon vegetable oil**
- 1 **package (16 ounces) frozen corn**
- ¼ **teaspoon salt**
- 1 **large avocado, diced**
- 1 **teaspoon lime juice**
- 1 **can (about 15 ounces) black beans, rinsed and drained**
- 2 **medium tomatoes, seeded and diced (1 cup)**
- ½ **cup finely chopped red onion**
- **Packaged tortilla strips or chips**
- **Chopped fresh lettuce or spinach**

1. For dressing, whisk mayonnaise, yogurt, 1 tablespoon lime juice, chili powder and garlic in small bowl. Stir in cheese and cilantro.

2. For salad, heat oil in saucepan over high heat. Add corn; cook 10 minutes or until lightly browned, stirring occasionally. Stir in salt. Remove to medium bowl; cool to room temperature. Combine avocado and 1 teaspoon lime juice in small bowl; toss to coat.

3. For each 1-quart jar, layer 2½ tablespoons dressing, ½ cup corn, scant ½ cup black beans, ¼ cup tomatoes, 2 tablespoons red onion and about ¼ cup avocado. Top with tortilla strips and lettuce. Seal jars.

4. Refrigerate until ready to serve.

NOTE: You can also make these without the lettuce. If so, use four (1-pint) jars.

BLACK BEAN AND BACON SOUP

MAKES 6 TO 8 SERVINGS

5 **strips bacon, sliced**

1 **medium onion, diced**

2 **tablespoons ORTEGA® Fire-Roasted Diced Green Chiles**

2 **cans (15 ounces each) ORTEGA® Black Beans, undrained**

4 **cups chicken broth**

½ **cup ORTEGA® Taco Sauce, any variety**

½ **cup sour cream**

4 **ORTEGA® Yellow Corn Taco Shells, crumbled**

Cook bacon in large pot over medium heat 5 minutes or until crisp. Add onion and chiles. Cook 5 minutes or until onion begins to brown. Stir in beans, broth and taco sauce. Bring to a boil. Reduce heat to low. Simmer 20 minutes.

Purée half of soup in food processor until smooth (or use immersion blender in pot). Return puréed soup to pot and stir to combine. Serve with dollop of sour cream and crumbled taco shells.

NOTE: For a less chunky soup, purée the entire batch and cook an additional 15 minutes.

BAKED POTATO SOUP

MAKES 8 SERVINGS

3 **cans (10³/₄ ounces each)
condensed cream of
mushroom soup**

4 **cups milk**

3 **cups diced peeled baked
potatoes**

¹/₂ **cup cooked crumbled bacon**

1 **tablespoon fresh thyme
leaves or 1 teaspoon dried
thyme leaves**

**Sour cream and shredded
Cheddar cheese**

1¹/₂ **cups FRENCH'S® French
Fried Onions**

1. Combine soup and milk in large saucepan until blended. Stir in potatoes, bacon and thyme. Cook over medium heat about 10 to 15 minutes or until heated through, stirring frequently. Season to taste with salt and pepper.

2. Ladle soup into serving bowls. Top with sour cream, cheese and 3 tablespoons French Fried Onions.

WEST AFRICAN PEANUT SOUP

MAKES 6 TO 8 SERVINGS

2 tablespoons vegetable oil

1 yellow or sweet onion, chopped

1/2 cup chopped roasted peanuts

1 1/2 tablespoons minced fresh ginger

4 cloves garlic, minced (about 1 tablespoon)

1 teaspoon salt

4 cups vegetable broth

2 sweet potatoes, peeled and cut into 1/2-inch cubes

1 can (28 ounces) whole tomatoes, drained and coarsely chopped

1/4 teaspoon ground red pepper

1 bunch Swiss chard or kale, stemmed and shredded

1/3 cup unsweetened peanut butter (creamy or chunky)

1. Heat oil in large saucepan over medium-high heat. Add onion; cook and stir 5 minutes or until softened. Add peanuts, ginger, garlic and salt; cook and stir 1 minute. Stir in broth, sweet potatoes, tomatoes and red pepper; bring to a boil. Reduce heat to medium; simmer 10 minutes.

2. Stir in kale and peanut butter; cook over medium-low heat 10 minutes or until vegetables are tender and soup is creamy.

BROCCOLI, CHEESE AND RICE SOUP

MAKES 6 SERVINGS

2 cups MINUTE® White or Brown Rice, uncooked

1 package (10 ounces) frozen chopped broccoli, thawed

1 can (10¾ ounces) reduced-fat cream of mushroom soup

3 cups low-fat milk

1 pound low-fat processed cheese, cubed

Shredded cheese (optional)

Prepare rice according to package directions.

Combine broccoli, soup and milk in medium saucepan. Bring to simmer over medium heat.

Add cheese and stir until melted. Remove from heat and stir in rice. Top with additional cheese, if desired.

OLD-FASHIONED SPLIT PEA SOUP

MAKES 8 SERVINGS

4 quarts chicken broth

2 pounds dried split peas, rinsed and sorted

1 cup chopped cooked ham

½ cup chopped onion

½ cup chopped celery

2 teaspoons salt

2 teaspoons black pepper

SLOW COOKER DIRECTIONS

Combine broth, peas, ham, onion, celery, salt and pepper in **CROCK-POT®** slow cooker; stir to blend. Cover; cook on LOW 8 to 10 hours or on HIGH 4 to 6 hours. Pour soup in batches into food processor or blender; purée until smooth.

CLASSIC ITALIAN PASTA SALAD

MAKES 8 SIDE-DISH SERVINGS

8 ounces rotelle or spiral pasta, cooked and drained

2½ cups assorted cut-up fresh vegetables (broccoli, carrots, tomatoes, bell peppers and onions)

½ cup cubed Cheddar or mozzarella cheese

⅓ cup sliced pitted ripe olives (optional)

1 cup WISH-BONE® Italian Dressing

Combine all ingredients except WISH-BONE® Italian Dressing in large bowl. Add Dressing; toss well. Serve chilled or at room temperature.

VARIATION: For a Creamy Italian Pasta Salad, substitute ½ cup HELLMANN'S® or BEST FOODS® Real Mayonnaise for ½ cup WISH-BONE® Italian Dressing.

SUBSTITUTION: Also terrific with WISH-BONE® Robusto Italian, Fat Free! Italian, House Italian, Ranch, Light Ranch, Fat-Free! Ranch, Creamy Caesar, Red Wine Vinaigrette or Fat Free! Red Wine Vinaigrette Dressings.

TIP

If preparing a day ahead, refrigerate, then stir in ¼ cup additional WISH-BONE® Dressing before serving.

CHOPPED SALAD WITH CORN BREAD CROUTONS

MAKES 8 SERVINGS

½ loaf Corn Bread (recipe follows),* cut into 1-inch cubes

1 large sweet potato, peeled and cut into 1-inch pieces

5 tablespoons olive oil, divided

1½ teaspoons salt, divided

3 tablespoons red wine vinegar

2 tablespoons white wine vinegar

1 tablespoon maple syrup

1 clove garlic, minced

1 teaspoon dried mustard

⅛ teaspoon dried oregano

Pinch red pepper flakes

½ cup vegetable oil

1 head iceberg lettuce

1 cup halved grape tomatoes

2 green onions, thinly sliced

1 avocado, diced

½ cup coarsely chopped smoked almonds

½ cup dried cranberries

1. Preheat oven to 400°F. Prepare Corn Bread. Cool in baking pan at least 10 minutes or cool completely; remove to cutting board. Cut half of corn bread into 1-inch cubes when cool enough to handle. Return to baking dish. *Reduce oven temperature to 350°F.* Bake 12 to 15 minutes or until corn bread is dry and toasted, stirring once.

2. Spread sweet potato in 13×9-inch baking pan. Drizzle with 1 tablespoon olive oil and sprinkle with ½ teaspoon salt; toss to coat. Bake 30 to 35 minutes or until browned and tender, stirring once or twice. Cool completely.

3. For dressing, whisk vinegars, maple syrup, garlic, mustard, oregano, red pepper flakes and remaining 1 teaspoon salt in medium bowl; whisk in remaining 4 tablespoons olive oil and vegetable oil in thin, steady stream.

4. Remove outer lettuce leaves and core. Chop lettuce into ½-inch pieces and place in large bowl. Add tomatoes, green onions and half of dressing; mix well. Add sweet potato, avocado, almonds and cranberries; mix well. Taste and add additional dressing, if desired. Add croutons; mix gently.

CORN BREAD | MAKES 12 SERVINGS

3 tablespoons boiling water

1 tablespoon ground flaxseed

1¼ cups all-purpose flour

¾ cup yellow cornmeal

⅓ cup sugar

2 teaspoons baking powder

1 teaspoon salt

1¼ cups plain unsweetened almond milk or soymilk

¼ cup vegetable oil

1. Preheat oven to 400°F. Spray 8-inch square baking dish or pan with nonstick cooking spray. Combine boiling water and flaxseed in small bowl; let stand until cool.

2. Combine flour, cornmeal, sugar, baking powder and salt in large bowl; mix well. Whisk almond milk and oil in medium bowl until well blended. Add to flour mixture with flaxseed mixture; stir just until dry ingredients are moistened. Pour batter into prepared baking dish.

3. Bake 25 minutes or until top is browned and toothpick inserted into center comes out clean.

CHICKEN NOODLE SOUP

MAKES 8 SERVINGS (10 CUPS)

2 tablespoons butter

1 cup chopped onion

1 cup sliced carrots

1/2 cup diced celery

2 tablespoons vegetable oil

1 pound chicken breast tenderloins

1 pound chicken thigh fillets

4 cups chicken broth, divided

2 cups water

1 tablespoon minced fresh parsley, plus additional for garnish

1 1/2 teaspoons salt

1/2 teaspoon black pepper

3 cups uncooked egg noodles

1. Melt butter in large saucepan or Dutch oven over medium-low heat. Add onion, carrots and celery; cook 15 minutes or until vegetables are soft, stirring occasionally.

2. Meanwhile, heat oil in large skillet over medium-high heat. Add chicken in single layer; cook 12 minutes or until lightly browned and cooked through, turning once. Transfer chicken to cutting board. Add 1 cup broth to skillet; cook 1 minute, scraping up any browned bits from bottom of skillet. Add broth to vegetables. Stir in remaining 3 cups broth, water, 1 tablespoon parsley, salt and pepper.

3. Chop chicken into 1-inch pieces when cool enough to handle. Add to soup; bring to a boil over medium-high heat. Reduce heat to medium-low; cook 15 minutes. Add noodles; cook 15 minutes or until noodles are tender. Ladle into bowls; garnish with additional parsley.

MARINATED BEAN AND VEGETABLE SALAD

MAKES 8 SERVINGS

¼ cup orange juice

3 tablespoons white wine vinegar

1 tablespoon canola or vegetable oil

2 cloves garlic, minced

1 can (about 15 ounces) Great Northern beans, rinsed and drained

1 can (about 15 ounces) kidney beans, rinsed and drained

¼ cup coarsely chopped red cabbage

¼ cup chopped red onion

¼ cup chopped green bell pepper

¼ cup chopped red bell pepper

¼ cup sliced celery

1. Combine orange juice, vinegar, oil and garlic in small jar with tight-fitting lid; shake well.

2. Combine beans, cabbage, onion, bell peppers and celery in large bowl. Pour dressing over bean mixture; toss to coat.

3. Refrigerate, covered, 1 to 2 hours to allow flavors to blend. Toss before serving.

TORTILLA SOUP

MAKES 4 SERVINGS

Vegetable oil

3 (6- or 7-inch) corn tortillas, halved and cut into strips

½ cup chopped onion

1 clove garlic, minced

2 cans (about 14 ounces each) chicken broth

1 can (about 14 ounces) diced tomatoes

1 cup shredded cooked chicken

2 teaspoons fresh lime juice

1 small avocado, diced

2 tablespoons chopped fresh cilantro

1. Pour oil to depth of ½ inch in small skillet. Heat over medium-high heat until oil reaches 360°F on deep-fry thermometer. Add tortilla strips, a few at a time; fry 1 minute or until crisp and lightly browned. Remove with slotted spoon; drain on paper towels.

2. Heat 2 teaspoons oil in large saucepan over medium heat. Add onion and garlic; cook and stir 6 to 8 minutes or until onion is softened. Add broth and tomatoes; bring to a boil. Cover; reduce heat to low. Simmer 15 minutes.

3. Add chicken and lime juice; simmer 5 minutes. Top soup with tortilla strips, avocado and cilantro.

COLORFUL COLESLAW

MAKES 4 TO 6 SERVINGS

¼ **head green cabbage, shredded or thinly sliced**

¼ **head red cabbage, shredded or thinly sliced**

1 **small yellow or orange bell pepper, thinly sliced**

1 **small jicama, peeled and julienned**

¼ **cup thinly sliced green onions**

2 **tablespoons chopped fresh cilantro**

¼ **cup vegetable oil**

¼ **cup fresh lime juice**

1 **teaspoon salt**

⅛ **teaspoon black pepper**

1. Combine cabbage, bell pepper, jicama, green onions and cilantro in large bowl.

2. Whisk oil, lime juice, salt and black pepper in small bowl until well blended. Pour over vegetables; toss to coat. Cover and refrigerate 2 to 6 hours for flavors to blend.

NOTE: This coleslaw makes a great topping for tacos and sandwiches.

RUSTIC VEGETABLE SOUP

MAKES 8 SERVINGS

- **1 to 2 baking potatoes, cut into ½-inch pieces**
- **1 bag (10 ounces) frozen mixed vegetables, thawed**
- **1 bag (10 ounces) frozen cut green beans, thawed**
- **1 medium green bell pepper, chopped**
- **1 jar (16 ounces) picante sauce**
- **1 can (about 10 ounces) condensed beef broth, undiluted**
- **½ teaspoon sugar**
- **¼ cup finely chopped fresh parsley**

SLOW COOKER DIRECTIONS

Combine potatoes, mixed vegetables, green beans, bell pepper, picante sauce, broth and sugar in slow cooker; stir to blend. Cover; cook on LOW 8 hours or on HIGH 4 hours. Stir in parsley just before serving.

CRUNCHY RAMEN CHICKEN SALAD

MAKES 4 SERVINGS

2 cups chopped cooked chicken (about 4 ounces)

1 package (8 ounces) broccoli slaw mix or coleslaw mix

1 can (11 ounces) mandarin oranges in light syrup, drained

¼ cup coleslaw dressing

1 package (3 ounces) ramen noodles, any flavor, crumbled*

*Discard seasoning packet.

1. Combine chicken, slaw mix, oranges and dressing in medium bowl. Cover and refrigerate until ready to serve.

2. Just before serving, add crumbled noodles. Stir to combine.

CHICKEN WALDORF SALAD

MAKES 4 SERVINGS

DRESSING

- 1/3 **cup balsamic vinegar**
- 2 **tablespoons Dijon mustard**
- 2 **teaspoons minced garlic**
- 1/2 **teaspoon salt**
- 1/4 **teaspoon black pepper**
- 2/3 **cup extra virgin olive oil**

SALAD

- 8 **cups mixed greens**
- 1 **large Granny Smith apple, cut into 1/2-inch pieces**
- 2/3 **cup diced celery**
- 2/3 **cup halved red seedless grapes**
- 12 **to 16 ounces sliced grilled chicken breasts**
- 1/2 **cup candied walnuts**
- 1/2 **cup crumbled blue cheese**

1. For dressing, combine vinegar, mustard, garlic, salt and pepper in medium bowl; mix well. Slowly add oil, whisking until well blended.

2. For salad, combine mixed greens, apple, celery and grapes in large bowl. Add half of dressing; toss to coat. Top with chicken, walnuts and cheese; drizzle with additional dressing.

DINNERTIME FAVORITES

SPICY SHREDDED BEEF TACOS

MAKES 6 TO 8 SERVINGS

1 **boneless beef chuck roast (2½ pounds)**

1¼ **teaspoons salt, divided**

1 **teaspoon *each* ground cumin, garlic powder and smoked paprika**

2 **tablespoons olive oil, divided**

2 **cups beef broth**

1 **red bell pepper, sliced**

1 **tomato, cut into wedges**

½ **onion, sliced**

2 **cloves garlic, minced**

1 **to 2 canned chipotle peppers in adobo sauce**

Juice of 1 lime

Corn or flour tortillas

Optional toppings: sliced bell peppers, avocado, diced onion, lime wedges and/or chopped fresh cilantro

SLOW COOKER DIRECTIONS

1. Season beef with 1 teaspoon salt, cumin, garlic powder and smoked paprika. Heat 1 tablespoon oil in large skillet over medium-high heat. Add beef; cook 5 minutes on each side until browned. Remove to slow cooker.

2. Pour in broth. Cover; cook on LOW 8 to 9 hours or on HIGH 4 to 5 hours.

3. Meanwhile, preheat oven to 425°F. Combine bell pepper, tomato, onion and garlic on large baking sheet. Drizzle with remaining 1 tablespoon oil. Roast 40 minutes or until vegetables are tender. Place vegetables, chipotle pepper, lime juice and remaining ¼ teaspoon salt in food processor or blender; blend until smooth.

4. Remove beef to large cutting board; shred with two forks. Combine shredded meat with 1 cup cooking liquid. Discard remaining cooking liquid. Serve on tortillas with sauce. Top as desired.

MEATBALL HERO SANDWICHES

MAKES 6 SERVINGS

1½ **pounds lean ground beef**

½ **cup Italian seasoned dry bread crumbs**

1 **egg**

1 **jar (1 pound 8 ounces) RAGÚ® Chunky Pasta Sauce**

6 **Italian rolls (about 6 inches long each), halved lengthwise**

½ **cup shredded part-skim mozzarella cheese (about 2 ounces)**

1. Combine ground beef, bread crumbs and egg in medium bowl; shape into 18 meatballs.

2. Bring RAGÚ® Chunky Pasta Sauce to a boil in 3-quart saucepan over medium-high heat. Gently stir in uncooked meatballs.

3. Reduce heat to low and simmer covered, stirring occasionally, 20 minutes or until meatballs are done. Serve meatballs and sauce in rolls; top with cheese.

TIP

Prepare extra meatball mixture and freeze it in individual portions. Then, for a last minute dinner, pull out and heat just what you need.

SWEET WINE AND MUSTARD HAM

MAKES 12 SERVINGS

¼ **cup butter**

½ **cup finely chopped onion**

1 **(750ml) bottle sweet white wine, divided**

¼ **cup honey**

1 **tablespoon thyme leaves**

2 **teaspoons crushed red pepper**

¾ **cup whole grain mustard**

1 **(16-pound) HORMEL® CURE 81® Bone-In Whole Ham**

1. In small skillet, melt butter over medium heat. Add onion and cook 5 minutes or until softened.

2. Add 1 cup wine, honey, thyme and crushed red peppers. Simmer 8 to 10 minutes or until reduced by half.

3. Remove from heat. Stir in mustard. Divide mixture in half.

4. Heat ham according to package directions. Use remaining wine instead of water in pan. Baste ham with one half of mustard mixture and wine from pan during cooking.

5. Serve ham with remaining mustard mixture.

CHILI AND CHEESE "BAKED" POTATO SUPPER

MAKES 12 SERVINGS

4 **russet potatoes (about 2 pounds)**

2 **cups prepared chili**

½ **cup (2 ounces) shredded Cheddar cheese**

4 **tablespoons sour cream (optional)**

2 **green onions, sliced**

SLOW COOKER DIRECTIONS

1. Prick potatoes in several places with fork. Wrap potatoes in aluminum foil. Place in slow cooker. Cover; cook on LOW 8 to 10 hours or on HIGH 4 to 5 hours. Carefully unwrap potatoes and place on serving dish.

2. Heat chili in microwave or on stovetop. Split hot potatoes and spoon chili on top. Sprinkle with cheese, sour cream, if desired, and green onions.

CRANBERRY-GLAZED TURKEY

MAKES 8 SERVINGS (1$\frac{1}{2}$ CUPS GLAZE)

- **1 whole turkey breast (about 5 pounds)**
- **Salt and pepper**
- **1 container (12 ounces) cran-orange cranberry sauce**
- **2 green onions, cut into 1-inch pieces**
- **2 tablespoons honey**
- **2 tablespoons FRANK'S® REDHOT® Original Cayenne Pepper Sauce**
- **1 tablespoon balsamic vinegar**
- **1 teaspoon rubbed sage**
- **$\frac{1}{4}$ teaspoon ground cloves**

PREHEAT oven to 350°F. Place turkey on greased rack in roasting pan. Season turkey with salt and pepper. Bake 2 hours and 15 minutes or until turkey is no longer pink near bone and meat thermometer inserted in thickest part of breast registers 170°F.

COMBINE remaining ingredients in blender or food processor. Cover; process until smooth. Generously baste turkey with glaze during last half hour of baking. Heat remaining glaze and serve with turkey.

BEEF CHILI FIVE WAYS

MAKES 4 SERVINGS

1 **pound Ground Beef (93% lean or leaner)**

1 **can (15½ ounces) black beans, rinsed and drained**

1 **can (14 to 14½-ounces) reduced-sodium or regular beef broth**

1 **can (14½ ounces) diced tomatoes with green chiles**

2 **tablespoons chili powder**

TOPPINGS:

Shredded Cheddar cheese, chopped fresh cilantro and/or minced green onion (optional)

1. Heat large nonstick skillet over medium heat until hot. Add Ground Beef; cook 8 to 10 minutes, breaking into ¾-inch crumbles and stirring occasionally. Pour off drippings.

2. Stir in beans, broth, tomatoes and chili powder; bring to a boil. Reduce heat. Cover and simmer 20 minutes to develop flavors, stirring occasionally. Garnish with Toppings, as desired.

MOROCCAN CHILI: Prepare recipe as directed above, adding ¼ teaspoon pumpkin pie spice and ¼ cup chopped pitted dates or golden raisins with ingredients in step 2. Serve over hot cooked couscous. Garnish with toasted sliced almonds, chopped fresh mint and Greek yogurt, as desired.

MEXICAN CHILI: Prepare recipe as directed above, adding 1 tablespoon cocoa powder with ingredients in step 2. Garnish with chopped fresh cilantro, pepitas (pumpkin seeds) and corn tortilla chips, as desired. Serve with corn tortillas.

ITALIAN CHILI: Prepare recipe as directed above, adding 1½ teaspoons fennel seed with ingredients in step 2. Before removing from heat, stir in 3 cups fresh baby spinach. Cover; turn off heat and let stand 3 to 5 minutes or until spinach is just wilted. Serve over hot cooked orecchiette or cavatappi, if desired. Garnish with grated Parmesan cheese and pine nuts, as desired.

CINCINNATI CHILI: Prepare recipe as directed above, adding 3 tablespoons white vinegar and 1 teaspoon ground cinnamon with ingredients in step 2. Serve over hot cooked elbow macaroni. Garnish with chopped white onion, sour cream and shredded Cheddar cheese, as desired.

VARIATIONS: One can (14½ ounces) diced tomatoes combined with 2 tablespoons diced canned chiles may be substituted for diced tomatoes with green chiles. And for a thicker consistency, prepare as directed, adding 1 tablespoon cornmeal with ingredients in step 2.

NOTE: Cooking times are for fresh or thoroughly thawed Ground Beef. Ground beef should be cooked to an internal temperature of 160°F. Color is not a reliable indicator of Ground Beef doneness.

COURTESY THE BEEF CHECKOFF

SCALLOP AND ARTICHOKE HEART CASSEROLE

MAKES 4 SERVINGS

1 **package (9 ounces) frozen artichoke hearts, cooked and drained**

1 **pound scallops**

1 **teaspoon canola or vegetable oil**

¼ **cup chopped red bell pepper**

¼ **cup sliced green onions**

¼ **cup all-purpose flour**

2 **cups milk**

1 **teaspoon dried tarragon**

¼ **teaspoon salt**

¼ **teaspoon white pepper**

1 **tablespoon chopped fresh parsley**

Dash paprika

1. Preheat oven to 350°F.

2. Cut large artichoke hearts lengthwise into halves; arrange in even layer in 8-inch square baking dish.

3. Rinse scallops; pat dry with paper towel. If scallops are large, cut into halves. Arrange scallops evenly over artichokes.

4. Heat oil in medium saucepan over medium-low heat. Add bell pepper and green onions; cook and stir 5 minutes or until tender. Stir in flour. Gradually stir in milk until smooth. Add tarragon, salt and white pepper; cook and stir over medium heat 10 minutes or until sauce boils and thickens. Pour sauce over scallops.

5. Bake, uncovered, 25 minutes or until casserole is bubbly and scallops are opaque. Sprinkle with parsley and paprika before serving.

TIP

White pepper is a mild version of the common black pepper. They both originate from the same berries, which are called peppercorns. White pepper helps to maintain consistent color in light foods.

CHICKEN BROCCOLI RICE CASSEROLE

MAKES 4 TO 6 SERVINGS

3 cups cooked long grain rice

4 boneless skinless chicken breasts (about 1 pound), cooked and cut into 1-inch pieces

1½ pounds broccoli, cut into 1-inch pieces and steamed until tender

2 cans (10¾ ounces each) condensed cream of celery soup, undiluted

¾ cup mayonnaise

½ cup whole milk

2 teaspoons curry powder

3 cups (12 ounces) shredded sharp Cheddar cheese

1. Preheat oven to 350°F. Grease 13×9-inch baking dish.

2. Spread cooked rice evenly into prepared dish. Top with chicken and broccoli. Mix soup, mayonnaise, milk and curry powder in medium bowl; pour over chicken and broccoli. Top with cheese.

3. Cover loosely with foil. Bake 45 minutes or until cheese is melted and casserole is heated through.

SEAFOOD NEWBURG CASSEROLE

MAKES 6 SERVINGS

1 **can (10¾ ounces) condensed cream of shrimp soup, undiluted**

½ **cup half-and-half**

1 **tablespoon dry sherry**

¼ **teaspoon ground red pepper**

2 **cans (6 ounces each) lump crabmeat, drained**

3 **cups cooked rice**

¼ **pound medium raw shrimp, peeled**

¼ **pound bay scallops, rinsed and patted dry**

1 **jar (4 ounces) pimientos, drained and chopped**

¼ **cup finely chopped fresh parsley**

1. Preheat oven to 350°F. Spray 2½-quart casserole with nonstick cooking spray.

2. Whisk soup, half-and-half, sherry and red pepper in large bowl until blended. Pick out and discard any shell or cartilage from crabmeat. Add crabmeat, rice, shrimp, scallops and pimientos to soup mixture; mix well. Transfer mixture to prepared casserole.

3. Bake, covered, 25 minutes or until shrimp and scallops are opaque. Sprinkle with parsley.

CHICKEN ZUCCHINI CASSEROLE

MAKES 8 SERVINGS

1 package (about 6 ounces) herb-flavored stuffing mix

½ cup (1 stick) butter, melted

2 cups cubed zucchini

1½ cups chopped cooked chicken

1 can (10¾ ounces) condensed cream of celery soup, undiluted

1 cup grated carrots

1 onion, chopped

½ cup sour cream

½ cup (2 ounces) shredded Cheddar cheese

1. Preheat oven to 350°F. Combine stuffing mix and butter in medium bowl; reserve 1 cup stuffing. Place remaining stuffing in 13×9-inch baking dish.

2. Combine zucchini, chicken, soup, carrots, onion and sour cream in large bowl; mix well. Pour over stuffing in baking dish; top with reserved 1 cup stuffing and cheese.

3. Bake 40 to 45 minutes or until heated through and cheese is melted.

ITALIAN BEEF

MAKES 8 SERVINGS

1 beef rump roast (3 to 5 pounds)*

1 can (14 ounces) beef broth

2 cups mild giardiniera

8 Italian bread rolls

Unless you have a 5-, 6- or 7-quart slow cooker, cut any roast larger than 2½ pounds in half so it cooks completely.

SLOW COOKER DIRECTIONS

1. Place rump roast in slow cooker; add broth and giardiniera.

2. Cover; cook on LOW 10 hours.

3. Shred beef; serve with sauce on crusty Italian rolls.

TUNA TOMATO CASSEROLE

MAKES 6 SERVINGS

2 cans (6 ounces each) tuna, drained and flaked

1 cup mayonnaise

1 onion, finely chopped

¼ teaspoon salt

¼ teaspoon black pepper

1 package (12 ounces) wide egg noodles, uncooked

8 to 10 plum tomatoes, sliced ¼ inch thick

1 cup (4 ounces) shredded Cheddar or mozzarella cheese

1. Preheat oven to 375°F.

2. Combine tuna, mayonnaise, onion, salt and pepper in medium bowl; mix well.

3. Cook noodles according to package directions; drain and return to saucepan. Gently stir in tuna mixture until well blended. Layer half of noodle mixture, half of tomatoes and half of cheese in 13×9-inch baking dish; press down slightly. Repeat layers.

4. Bake 20 minutes or until cheese is melted and casserole is heated through.

SMOTHERED BEEF AND SAUSAGE MEATBALL SANDWICHES

MAKES 4 TO 6 SERVINGS

12 **ounces sweet or hot Italian sausages, casings removed**

12 **ounces ground beef**

1 **onion, minced**

1/3 **cup Italian seasoned dry bread crumbs**

1/3 **cup grated Parmesan cheese**

1 **egg, beaten**

1/4 **teaspoon black pepper**

2 **tablespoons olive oil**

1 **onion, sliced**

1 **red bell pepper, sliced**

2 **cloves garlic, minced**

1 **cup lager**

1 **tablespoon tomato paste**

4 **to 6 crusty rolls, split lengthwise**

1. Preheat oven to 350°F. Spray baking sheet with nonstick cooking spray.

2. Combine sausages, beef, minced onion, bread crumbs, cheese, egg and black pepper in medium bowl. Shape into 16 meatballs. Place on prepared baking sheet. Bake 20 minutes or until browned.

3. Heat oil in large skillet over medium heat. Add sliced onion, bell pepper and garlic; cook and stir 5 minutes or until softened. Stir in lager and tomato paste; bring to a boil. Add meatballs and partially cover. Reduce heat to low; simmer 20 minutes or until liquid is reduced to 2 tablespoons and vegetables are tender.

4. Preheat broiler. Broil rolls 2 minutes or until lightly toasted. Divide meatballs and vegetables evenly among rolls. Serve immediately.

TIP
To make these sandwiches a little less messy, pull some of the bread from each roll to make a trough for the meatballs and vegetables.

BEEF STROGANOFF CASSEROLE

MAKES 6 SERVINGS

1 pound ground beef

¼ teaspoon salt

⅛ teaspoon black pepper

1 teaspoon vegetable oil

8 ounces sliced mushrooms

1 large onion, chopped

3 cloves garlic, minced

¼ cup dry white wine

1 can (10¾ ounces) condensed cream of mushroom soup, undiluted

½ cup sour cream

1 tablespoon Dijon mustard

4 cups cooked egg noodles

Chopped fresh parsley (optional)

1. Preheat oven to 350°F. Spray 13×9-inch baking dish with nonstick cooking spray.

2. Place beef in large skillet; season with salt and pepper. Brown beef over medium-high heat 6 to 8 minutes, stirring to break up meat. Drain fat. Remove beef from skillet and set aside.

3. Heat oil in same skillet over medium-high heat. Add mushrooms, onion and garlic; cook and stir 2 minutes or until onion is tender. Add wine. Reduce heat to medium-low and simmer 3 minutes. Remove from heat; stir in soup, sour cream and mustard until well blended. Return beef to skillet; stir to blend.

4. Place noodles in prepared dish. Pour beef mixture over noodles; stir until noodles are well coated.

5. Bake 30 minutes or until heated through. Sprinkle with parsley, if desired.

IT'S A KEEPER CASSEROLE

MAKES 4 SERVINGS

1 tablespoon vegetable oil

½ cup chopped onion

¼ cup chopped green bell pepper

1 clove garlic, minced

2 tablespoons all-purpose flour

1 teaspoon sugar

½ teaspoon salt

½ teaspoon dried basil

½ teaspoon black pepper

1 package (about 16 ounces) frozen meatballs, thawed

1 can (about 14 ounces) whole tomatoes, cut up and drained

1½ cups cooked vegetables (any combination)

1 teaspoon beef bouillon granules

1 teaspoon Worcestershire sauce

1 can (12 ounces) refrigerated buttermilk biscuits

1. Preheat oven to 400°F. Heat oil in large saucepan over medium heat. Add onion, bell pepper and garlic; cook and stir until vegetables are tender.

2. Stir in flour, sugar, salt, basil and black pepper; mix well. Add meatballs, tomatoes, vegetables, bouillon and Worcestershire sauce. Cook and stir until slightly thickened and bubbly. Pour into 2-quart casserole.

3. Place biscuits on top of casserole. Bake 15 minutes or until biscuits are golden brown.

VARIATION: You may also use ground beef or sliced hot dogs in place of the frozen meatballs.

VEGETARIAN CHILI

MAKES 8 TO 10 SERVINGS

2 tablespoons olive oil

1 onion, finely chopped

2 medium carrots, chopped

1 red bell pepper, chopped

3 tablespoons chili powder

2 tablespoons ground cumin

2 tablespoons tomato paste

2 tablespoons packed dark
    brown sugar

3 cloves garlic, minced

1 tablespoon dried oregano

1 teaspoon salt

1 can (28 ounces) diced
    tomatoes

1 can (15 ounces) tomato
    sauce

1 can (about 15 ounces) small
    white beans, rinsed and
    drained

1 can (about 15 ounces) light
    kidney beans, rinsed and
    drained

1 can (about 15 ounces) dark
    kidney beans, rinsed and
    drained

1 can (about 15 ounces) pinto
    beans, rinsed and drained

1 cup vegetable broth

1 can (4 ounces) diced mild
    green chiles

1 ounce unsweetened baking
    chocolate, chopped

1 tablespoon cider vinegar

1. Heat oil in large saucepan or Dutch oven over medium-high heat. Add onion, carrots and bell pepper; cook 10 minutes or until vegetables are tender, stirring frequently. Add chili powder, cumin, tomato paste, brown sugar, garlic, oregano and salt; cook and stir 1 minute.

2. Stir in tomatoes, tomato sauce, beans, broth, chiles and chocolate; bring to a boil. Reduce heat to medium; simmer 20 minutes, stirring occasionally. Stir in vinegar.

SUMMER FIESTA CASSEROLE

MAKES 4 TO 6 SERVINGS

2 **pounds ground beef**

1 **medium onion, chopped**

1 **package (about 1 ounce) taco seasoning mix**

4 **to 6 potatoes, peeled and cut into ½-inch cubes (about 4 cups)**

1 **to 2 tablespoons vegetable oil**

4 **cups sliced zucchini**

1 **can (about 14 ounces) diced tomatoes with onion and garlic**

1½ **cups (6 ounces) shredded Mexican cheese blend**

1. Preheat oven to 350°F. Spray 4-quart casserole with nonstick cooking spray.

2. Brown beef and onion in large skillet over medium heat 6 to 8 minutes, stirring to break up meat. Drain fat. Add taco seasoning mix and cook 5 minutes, stirring occasionally. Transfer meat mixture to prepared casserole.

3. Add potatoes to same skillet; cook and stir over medium heat until potatoes are browned, adding oil as needed to prevent sticking. Add zucchini; cook and stir until beginning to soften. Transfer to casserole; top with tomatoes and cheese.

4. Bake 10 to 15 minutes or until cheese is melted and casserole is heated through.

SERVING SUGGESTIONS: Serve with tortilla chips, sour cream and/or salsa.

CHICKEN CHILE RELLENO CASSEROLE

MAKES 6 SERVINGS

- **3 cups diced cooked chicken**
- **1 can (about 7 ounces) chopped green chiles**
- **1½ cups shredded pepper-jack or Mexican cheese blend, divided**
- **1½ cups salsa, divided**
- **¾ cup milk**
- **3 eggs**
- **¼ cup all-purpose flour**
- **1 teaspoon chili powder**
- **2 tablespoons minced fresh cilantro**

1. Preheat oven to 350°F. Spray 2-quart casserole with nonstick cooking spray.

2. Spread chicken in casserole; top with chiles and ¾ cup cheese. Whisk together ½ cup salsa, milk, eggs, flour and chili powder in medium bowl. Stir in ¼ cup cheese; pour over chicken.

3. Sprinkle with remaining ½ cup cheese. Bake 25 to 30 minutes or until set and cheese is lightly browned. Sprinkle with cilantro and serve with remaining 1 cup salsa.

HOGS IN A BLANKET

MAKES 6 SERVINGS

½ **of a (17.3 ounce package) PEPPERIDGE FARM® Frozen Puff Pastry Sheets (1 sheet)**

6 **(10-inch long) wooden skewers**

6 **(6- to 7-inch long) frankfurters (12 ounces)**

1 **jar (11 ounces) PACE® Picante Sauce**

1 **can (10¾ ounces) CAMPBELL'S® Condensed Cream of Celery Soup (Regular OR 98% Fat Free)**

1 **cup shredded Cheddar cheese (4 ounces)**

1. Thaw the pastry sheet at room temperature for 40 minutes or until it's easy to handle. Heat the oven to 400°F. Lightly grease a baking sheet.

2. Insert the skewers into the frankfurters, leaving 3 inches of wood exposed.

3. Unfold the pastry sheet on a lightly floured surface. Roll the sheet into a 12X10-inch rectangle. Cut the pastry crosswise into 6 (2-inch) strips. Starting at one end, wrap a pastry strip around a frankfurter overlapping the pastry slightly while winding it around the frankfurter to the other end, pressing lightly to seal. Place on the baking sheet. Repeat with remaining pastry strips and frankfurters.

4. Bake for 25 minutes or until golden brown.

5. Mix the picante sauce, soup and cheese in a 2-quart saucepan. Cook over medium heat until it's hot and the cheese melts. Serve the frankfurters with the sauce mixture for dipping.

LAYERED PASTA CASSEROLE

MAKES 6 TO 8 SERVINGS

- 8 ounces uncooked penne pasta
- 8 ounces mild Italian sausage, casings removed
- 8 ounces ground beef
- 1 jar (about 26 ounces) pasta sauce
- 1 package (10 ounces) frozen chopped spinach, thawed and squeezed dry
- 2 cups (8 ounces) shredded mozzarella cheese, divided
- 1 cup ricotta cheese
- ½ cup grated Parmesan cheese
- 1 egg
- 2 tablespoons chopped fresh basil *or* 2 teaspoons dried basil
- 1 teaspoon salt

1. Preheat oven to 350°F. Spray 13×9-inch baking dish with nonstick cooking spray. Cook pasta according to package directions; drain. Transfer to prepared dish.

2. Brown sausage and beef in large skillet over medium-high heat 6 to 8 minutes, stirring to break up meat. Drain fat. Add pasta sauce; mix well. Add half of meat sauce to pasta; toss to coat.

3. Combine spinach, 1 cup mozzarella cheese, ricotta cheese, Parmesan cheese, egg, basil and salt in medium bowl. Spoon small mounds of spinach mixture over pasta mixture; spread evenly with back of spoon. Top with remaining meat sauce; sprinkle with remaining 1 cup mozzarella cheese.

4. Bake 30 minutes or until heated through.

TURKEY AND ALL THE FIXIN' TACOS

MAKES 8 TACOS

- **1 pound ground turkey**
- **1 packet (1.25 ounces) ORTEGA® Taco Seasoning Mix**
- **¼ cup ORTEGA® Salsa, any variety**
- **2 cups prepared mashed potatoes**
- **¼ cup shredded Cheddar cheese**
- **8 ORTEGA® Yellow Corn Taco Shells**
- **¼ cup cranberry sauce**

Heat turkey in large skillet over medium-heat 5 minutes, stirring to break up meat. Add taco seasoning mix, salsa and ¼ cup water, stirring to combine. Heat through 3 minutes. Combine mashed potatoes and cheese in large bowl; microwave 2 minutes to heat through. Fill each taco shell with ¼ cup mashed potatoes; top with turkey and dollop of cranberry sauce.

TIP

This recipe makes a great meal by allowing guests to build their own tacos with the ingredients separated in individual bowls. Try adding French fried onions for added crunch.

PULLED PORK SANDWICHES

MAKES 6 TO 8 SERVINGS

2 tablespoons kosher salt

2 tablespoons packed light brown sugar

2 tablespoons paprika

1 teaspoon dry mustard

1 teaspoon black pepper

1 boneless pork shoulder roast (about 3 pounds)

1 1/2 cups stout

1/2 cup cider vinegar

6 to 8 large hamburger buns, split

3/4 cup barbecue sauce

1. Preheat oven to 325°F. Combine salt, brown sugar, paprika, dry mustard and pepper in small bowl; mix well. Rub into pork.

2. Place pork in 4-quart Dutch oven. Add stout and vinegar. Cover; bake 3 hours or until meat is fork-tender. Remove to large cutting board. Cool 15 to 30 minutes or until cool enough to handle.

3. Shred pork into pieces with two forks. Divide onto buns; serve warm with barbecue sauce.

SERVING SUGGESTIONS: Baked beans, corn on the cob and watermelon are wonderful accompaniments.

HEARTY CHILI MAC

MAKES 4 SERVINGS

1 pound 90% lean ground beef

1 can (about 14 ounces) diced tomatoes, drained

1 cup chopped onion

1 tablespoon chili powder

1 clove garlic, minced

½ teaspoon salt

½ teaspoon ground cumin

½ teaspoon dried oregano

¼ teaspoon red pepper flakes

¼ teaspoon black pepper

2 cups cooked elbow macaroni

SLOW COOKER DIRECTIONS

1. Brown beef in large nonstick skillet over medium-high heat, stirring to break up meat. Drain fat. Add tomatoes, onion, chili powder, garlic, salt, cumin, oregano, red pepper flakes and black pepper to slow cooker; mix well.

2. Cover; cook on LOW 4 hours.

3. Stir in macaroni. Cover; cook on LOW 1 hour.

ON THE SIDE

APPLE AND CARROT CASSEROLE

MAKES 6 SERVINGS

6 **large carrots (about 1½ inches in diameter)**

4 **large Granny Smith apples, peeled**

¼ **cup all-purpose flour**

1 **tablespoon packed brown sugar**

½ **teaspoon salt**

½ **teaspoon ground nutmeg**

1 **tablespoon unsalted butter**

½ **cup orange juice**

1. Preheat oven to 350°F. Spiral carrots and apples with thick spiral blade.* Layer in 2-quart casserole.

2. Combine flour, brown sugar, salt and nutmeg in small bowl; cut in butter. Sprinkle over casserole and pour orange juice over topping.

3. Bake 30 minutes or until carrots and apples are tender.

If you don't have a spiralizer, cut the carrots and apples into thin strips.

JALAPEÑO AND PALE ALE CORN BREAD WITH HONEY BUTTER

MAKES 12 SERVINGS

1½ **cups all-purpose flour**

1½ **cups yellow cornmeal**

⅓ **cup sugar**

2 **teaspoons baking powder**

¾ **teaspoon salt**

½ **teaspoon baking soda**

1 **cup pale ale**

½ **cup corn oil**

½ **cup buttermilk**

2 **eggs**

2 **jalapeño peppers, finely chopped**

Honey Butter (recipe follows)

1. Preheat oven to 400°F. Butter 8-inch square baking pan.

2. Combine flour, cornmeal, sugar, baking powder, salt and baking soda in large bowl. Combine ale, oil, buttermilk, eggs and jalapeños in medium bowl. Stir ale mixture into flour mixture just until moistened. Pour batter into prepared baking pan.

3. Bake 25 to 27 minutes or until toothpick inserted into center comes out clean. Cool in pan 10 minutes. Prepare Honey Butter.

4. Cut corn bread into squares and serve warm with Honey Butter.

HONEY BUTTER: Combine 6 tablespoons softened unsalted butter, 2 tablespoons honey and ¼ teaspoon salt in small bowl; stir until smooth.

CHEESY SPINACH CASSEROLE

MAKES 6 SERVINGS

1 pound baby spinach

4 slices bacon, chopped

1 small onion, chopped

1 cup sliced mushrooms

1/4 cup chopped red bell pepper

3 cloves garlic, minced

1 1/2 teaspoons minced canned chipotle peppers in adobo sauce

1 teaspoon seasoned salt

8 ounces pasteurized process cheese product, cut into pieces

1/2 (8-ounce) package cream cheese, cut into pieces

1 cup thawed frozen corn

1/2 cup (2 ounces) shredded Monterey Jack and Cheddar cheese blend

1. Preheat oven to 350°F. Spray 1-quart baking dish with nonstick cooking spray.

2. Heat large saucepan of water to a boil over high heat. Add spinach; cook 1 minute. Drain and transfer to bowl of ice water to stop cooking. Drain and squeeze spinach dry; set aside. Wipe out saucepan with paper towel.

3. Cook bacon in same saucepan over medium-high heat until almost crisp, stirring frequently. Drain off all but 1 tablespoon drippings. Add onion to saucepan; cook and stir 3 minutes or until softened. Add mushrooms and bell pepper; cook and stir 5 minutes or until vegetables are tender. Add garlic, chipotle peppers and seasoned salt; cook and stir 1 minute.

4. Add cheese product and cream cheese to saucepan; cook over medium heat until melted, stirring frequently. Add spinach and corn; cook and stir 3 minutes. Transfer to prepared baking dish; sprinkle with shredded cheese.

5. Bake 20 to 25 minutes or until cheese is melted and casserole is bubbly. If desired, broil 1 to 2 minutes to brown top of casserole.

CREAMY LOADED MASHED POTATOES

MAKES 8 SERVINGS

3 pounds all-purpose potatoes, peeled and cubed

1½ cups shredded Cheddar cheese (about 6 ounces), divided

1 cup HELLMANN'S® or BEST FOODS® Real Mayonnaise

1 cup sour cream

3 green onions, finely chopped

6 slices bacon or turkey bacon, crisp-cooked and crumbled, divided (optional)

1. Preheat oven to 375°F. Spray 2-quart shallow baking dish with nonstick cooking spray; set aside.

2. Cover potatoes with water in 4-quart saucepot; bring to a boil over high heat. Reduce heat to low and cook 10 minutes or until potatoes are tender; drain and mash.

3. Stir in 1 cup cheese, HELLMANN'S® or BEST FOODS® Real Mayonnaise, sour cream, green onions and 4 slices crumbled bacon. Turn into prepared baking dish and bake 30 minutes or until bubbling.

4. Top with remaining ½ cup cheese and bacon. Bake an additional 5 minutes or until cheese is melted. Garnish, if desired, with additional chopped green onions.

CUBAN RICE & BEANS

MAKES 8 SERVINGS

2 tablespoons I CAN'T BELIEVE IT'S NOT BUTTER!® Light Spread, divided

1 cup finely chopped onion, divided

1 cup uncooked regular or converted rice

2 cups water

¼ teaspoon salt

¼ cup finely chopped green bell pepper

1 can (about 15 ounces) black beans, undrained

1 tablespoon chopped garlic

1 teaspoon dried oregano, crushed

Fresh cilantro (optional)

1. Melt 1 tablespoon I CAN'T BELIEVE IT'S NOT BUTTER!® Light Spread in 3-quart saucepan over medium heat and cook ½ cup onion, stirring occasionally, 3 minutes or until tender. Add rice and cook, stirring frequently, 2 minutes or until rice is golden. Add water and salt and bring to a boil over high heat. Reduce heat to low and simmer, covered, 20 minutes or until rice is tender.

2. Meanwhile, melt remaining 1 tablespoon Spread in 2-quart saucepan over medium heat and cook remaining ½ cup onion with bell pepper, stirring occasionally, 5 minutes or until vegetables are tender. Stir in remaining ingredients and bring to a boil over high heat. Reduce heat to low and simmer, stirring occasionally, 3 minutes.

3. Arrange rice on serving platter in a ring. Arrange vegetables in center of rice ring. Garnish, if desired, with cilantro.

TRUFFLE MACARONI AND CHEESE

MAKES 6 TO 8 SERVINGS

1 **pound uncooked ditalini pasta**

½ **cup (1 stick) butter, divided**

¼ **cup all-purpose flour**

4 **cups whole milk**

1 **teaspoon salt**

¼ **teaspoon ground nutmeg**

8 **ounces smoked mozzarella, shredded**

5 **ounces fontina cheese, shredded**

5 **ounces Asiago cheese, shredded**

4 **ounces Cheddar cheese, shredded**

½ **cup grated Romano cheese**

2 **tablespoons truffle oil**

1 **clove garlic, minced**

¼ **teaspoon Italian seasoning**

4 **cups cubed French bread (½-inch cubes)**

1. Preheat oven to 375°F. Cook pasta in large saucepan of salted water 9 minutes or until al dente. Drain and set aside.

2. Melt ¼ cup butter in large saucepan over medium heat. Add flour; whisk until smooth and well blended. Slowly whisk in milk in thin, steady stream. Add salt and nutmeg; cook 7 minutes or until thickened, whisking frequently.

3. Combine mozzarella, fontina, Asiago and Cheddar cheeses in large bowl; reserve 1½ cups for topping. Gradually add remaining cheese mixture by handfuls to milk mixture, whisking until smooth after each addition. Stir in Romano cheese until blended. Stir in truffle oil. Add pasta; stir until well blended. Spread in 2-quart baking dish or individual baking dishes; top with reserved cheese mixture.

4. Melt remaining ¼ cup butter in large skillet over medium-high heat. Add garlic and Italian seasoning; cook and stir 30 seconds or until garlic is fragrant but not browned. Add bread cubes; stir to coat. Spread over top of pasta.

5. Bake 20 minutes or until cheese is bubbly and bread cubes are golden brown.

ARIZONA RANCH BEANS

MAKES 6 TO 8 SERVINGS

1 **pound dried pinto beans, rinsed and sorted**

8 **cups water, plus more for soaking**

½ **pound bacon, diced**

1 **can (about 14 ounces) whole tomatoes, undrained and coarsely chopped**

2 **medium onions, chopped**

2 **cloves garlic, minced**

1 **can (4 ounces) diced mild green chiles**

1 **teaspoon chili powder**

½ **teaspoon dried oregano**

¼ **teaspoon ground cumin**

Salt

2 **limes, cut into wedges**

1. Place beans in large Dutch oven. Add enough water to cover beans by 2 inches. Cover; bring to a boil over high heat. Boil 2 minutes. Remove from heat; let soak, covered, 1 hour. Drain.

2. Add 8 cups water. Simmer, partially covered, 1 hour. Cook bacon in large skillet until crisp. Add bacon and 2 tablespoons drippings to beans. Add tomatoes, onions, garlic, chiles, chili powder, oregano and cumin. Simmer, partially covered, 3 hours or until beans are very tender. At end of cooking, beans should have a little liquid. If beans become too dry, add more water. If beans have more liquid than desired, uncover and boil over medium heat. Cook and stir 3 to 5 minutes or until mixture is thickened.

3. Season with salt. Serve with lime wedges.

MINI MACARONI & CHEESE CUPS

MAKES 4 SERVINGS

- **3 tablespoons plain dry bread crumbs**
- **1 teaspoon butter, melted**
- **1 can (10¾ ounces) CAMPBELL'S® Condensed Cheddar Cheese Soup**
- **2 tablespoons milk**
- **⅛ teaspoon ground black pepper**
- **2 cups cooked rotini (spiral) pasta or medium shell-shaped pasta, cooked and drained**
- **1 cup shredded Cheddar cheese (about 4 ounces)**

1. Heat the oven to 400°F. Spray 8 (2½-inch) muffin-pan cups with vegetable cooking spray and lightly coat with 1 tablespoon bread crumbs. Stir the remaining bread crumbs and the butter in a small bowl.

2. Stir the soup, milk, black pepper, rotini and ¾ cup cheese in a medium bowl. Spoon about ⅓ cup rotini mixture into each muffin-pan cup. Sprinkle with the remaining cheese and bread crumb mixture.

3. Bake for 20 minutes or until the rotini mixture is hot and bubbling. Let stand for 10 minutes before removing the minis from the pan.

COUNTRY-STYLE CORN

MAKES 6 TO 8 SERVINGS

4 **slices bacon**

1 **tablespoon all-purpose flour**

1 **can (about 15 ounces) corn, drained**

1 **can (about 15 ounces) cream-style corn**

1 **red bell pepper, diced**

½ **cup sliced green onions**

Salt and black pepper

1. Cook bacon in large skillet over medium heat until crisp; drain on paper towels. Crumble bacon; set aside.

2. Whisk flour into drippings in skillet. Add corn, cream-style corn and bell pepper; bring to a boil. Reduce heat to low. Cook 10 minutes or until thickened.

3. Stir green onions and bacon into corn mixture. Season with salt and black pepper.

CHEDDAR BROCCOLI CASSEROLE WITH CRUNCHY TOPPING

MAKES 8 SERVINGS

1 can (10¾ ounces) condensed cream of mushroom soup

1 cup (4 ounces) shredded Cheddar cheese

2 eggs

¼ cup plain nonfat Greek yogurt

1 teaspoon salt

1 can (5 ounces) sliced water chestnuts, drained

½ cup chopped onion

2 packages (9 ounces each) frozen chopped broccoli, thawed

8 round butter crackers, crushed

2 teaspoons unsalted butter, melted

1. Preheat oven to 350°F. Spray 2-quart casserole with nonstick cooking spray.

2. Combine soup, cheese, eggs, yogurt and salt in large bowl; mix well. Stir in water chestnuts and onion. Fold in broccoli. Pour into prepared casserole.

3. Bake 30 minutes.

4. Meanwhile, combine crackers and butter in small bowl; sprinkle evenly over casserole. Bake 5 minutes or until lightly browned. Let stand 10 minutes before serving.

RUSTIC GARLIC MASHED POTATOES

MAKES 6 SERVINGS

2 **pounds baking potatoes, cut into ½-inch cubes**

¼ **cup water**

2 **tablespoons butter, cut into small pieces**

1¼ **teaspoons salt**

½ **teaspoon garlic powder**

¼ **teaspoon black pepper**

1 **cup milk**

SLOW COOKER DIRECTIONS

1. Place potatoes, water, butter, salt, garlic powder and pepper in slow cooker; mix well. Cover; cook on LOW 7 hours or on HIGH 4 hours.

2. Add milk; mash potatoes with potato masher or electric mixer until smooth.

HONEY-GLAZED CARROTS

MAKES 4 SERVINGS

1 **pound carrots, sliced**

3 **tablespoons COUNTRY CROCK® Honey Spread or COUNTRY CROCK® Spread, divided**

¼ **cup finely chopped onion**

2 **teaspoons sugar**

¼ **teaspoon salt**

1. Cover carrots with 1-inch water in 10-inch nonstick skillet. Bring to a boil over high heat. Reduce heat to low and simmer covered until crisp-tender, about 8 minutes; drain.

2. Return carrots to skillet. Add 2 tablespoons COUNTRY CROCK® Honey Spread and remaining ingredients and cook, stirring occasionally, until carrots are tender, about 5 minutes. To serve, top with remaining 1 tablespoon Spread.

90-MINUTE DINNER ROLLS

MAKES 12 ROLLS

- **2 to 2¼ cups all-purpose flour, divided**
- **1 envelope FLEISCHMANN'S® RapidRise Yeast**
- **2 tablespoons sugar**
- **½ teaspoon salt**
- **½ cup milk**
- **¼ cup water**
- **2 tablespoons butter or margarine**

COMBINE ¾ cup flour, undissolved yeast, sugar and salt in a large mixing bowl. Heat milk, water and butter until very warm (120° to 130°F). Add to flour mixture. Beat 2 minutes at medium speed with electric mixer, scraping bowl occasionally. Add ¼ cup flour; beat 2 minutes at high speed. Stir in enough remaining flour to make a soft dough. Knead on lightly floured surface until smooth and elastic, about 8 to 10 minutes. Cover; let rest 10 minutes.

DIVIDE dough into 12 equal pieces; shape into balls. Place in greased 8-inch round pan. Cover; let rise in warm, draft-free place until doubled in size, about 30 minutes.

BAKE in preheated 375°F oven for 20 minutes or until done. Remove from pan; brush with additional melted butter, if desired. Serve warm.

FRIJOLES BORRACHOS (DRUNKEN BEANS)

MAKES 8 SERVINGS

6 slices bacon, chopped

1 medium yellow onion, chopped

1 tablespoon minced garlic

3 jalapeño peppers,* seeded and finely diced

1 tablespoon dried oregano

1 can (12 ounces) beer

6 cups water

1 pound dried pinto beans, rinsed and sorted

1 can (about 14 ounces) diced tomatoes

1 tablespoon kosher salt

¼ cup chopped fresh cilantro

Jalapeño peppers can sting and irritate the skin, so wear rubber gloves when handling peppers and do not touch your eyes.

SLOW COOKER DIRECTIONS

1. Heat large skillet over medium-high heat. Add bacon; cook 5 minutes or until mostly browned and crisp. Remove to slow cooker. Discard all but 3 tablespoons of drippings.

2. Heat same skillet over medium heat. Add onion; cook 6 minutes or until softened and lightly browned. Add garlic, jalapeños and oregano; cook 30 seconds or until fragrant. Increase heat to medium-high. Add beer; bring to a simmer. Cook 2 minutes, stirring and scraping any brown bits from bottom of skillet. Remove mixture to slow cooker.

3. Add water, beans, tomatoes and salt to slow cooker. Cover; cook on LOW 8 hours or on HIGH 6 hours or until beans are tender. Mash beans slightly until broth is thickened and creamy. Stir in cilantro.

ZUCCHINI WITH FETA CASSEROLE

MAKES 4 SERVINGS

4 **medium zucchini**

1 **tablespoon butter**

2 **eggs, beaten**

½ **cup grated Parmesan cheese**

⅓ **cup crumbled feta cheese**

2 **tablespoons chopped fresh parsley**

1 **tablespoon all-purpose flour**

2 **teaspoons chopped fresh marjoram**

Dash hot pepper sauce

Salt and black pepper

1. Preheat oven to 375°F. Spray 2-quart casserole with nonstick cooking spray.

2. Grate zucchini; drain in colander. Melt butter in large skillet over medium heat. Add zucchini; cook and stir until slightly browned.

3. Remove from heat; stir in eggs, cheeses, parsley, flour, marjoram, hot pepper sauce, salt and black pepper until well blended. Pour into prepared casserole.

4. Bake 35 minutes or until hot and bubbly.

COLA MASHED SWEET POTATOES

MAKES 4 SERVINGS

2 **large sweet potatoes, cubed**

¼ **cup cola beverage**

3 **tablespoons butter**

¼ **teaspoon ground nutmeg**
   Salt and black pepper

1. Cook potatoes in salted boiling water in large saucepan until tender, about 20 minutes; drain.

2. Add cola and butter; mash.

3. Stir in nutmeg; season with salt and pepper.

CLASSIC POLENTA

MAKES 6 TO 8 SERVINGS

6 **cups water**

2 **teaspoons salt**

2 **cups yellow cornmeal**

¼ **cup vegetable oil**

1. Bring water and salt to a boil in large heavy saucepan over medium-high heat. Stirring water vigorously, add cornmeal in very thin but steady stream (do not let lumps form). Reduce heat to low.

2. Cook polenta, uncovered, about 30 minutes or until thick and creamy, stirring frequently. Serve at this point for soft polenta. (See Tips.)

3. For firm polenta, cook 10 to 20 minutes longer or until very thick. Polenta is ready when spoon will stand upright by itself in center of mixture. Spray 11×7-inch baking pan with nonstick cooking spray. Spread polenta evenly in baking pan. Cover; refrigerate until completely cooled and firm.

4. To serve fried, unmold polenta from baking pan onto cutting board. Cut polenta crosswise into 1¼-inch-wide strips. Cut strips into 2- to 3-inch-long pieces.

5. Heat oil in large heavy skillet over medium-high heat; reduce heat to medium. Fry polenta pieces, half at a time, 4 to 5 minutes or until golden on all sides, turning as needed. Serve warm; garnish as desired.

TIPS

Polenta is an important component of Northern Italian cooking. The basic preparation presented here can be served in two forms. Hot freshly made polenta, prepared through step 2, can be mixed with ⅓ cup butter and ⅓ cup grated Parmesan cheese and served as a first course. Or, pour onto a large platter and top with a hearty meat or vegetable sauce for a main dish. Fried polenta can be served as an appetizer or as a side dish; cut into strips or rounds. Polenta also can be baked, broiled or grilled.

PARMESAN-PEPPER CLOVERLEAF ROLLS

MAKES 12 SERVINGS

- ¾ **cup plus 2 tablespoons grated Parmesan cheese, divided**
- ½ **teaspoon black pepper**
- 1 **loaf (16 ounces) frozen bread dough, thawed**

1. Knead ¾ cup cheese and pepper into dough, adding cheese 2 to 3 tablespoons at a time, until evenly mixed. Divide dough into 12 equal pieces; shape into balls. Cover with plastic wrap; let rest 10 minutes.

2. Coat 12 standard (2½-inch) muffin cups and hands with nonstick cooking spray. Divide each ball of dough into 3 pieces. Roll each piece into small ball. Place 3 balls in each muffin cup. Cover rolls loosely with plastic wrap; let rise in warm place (85°F) 30 minutes or until doubled in size.

3. Preheat oven to 350°F. Sprinkle rolls with remaining 2 tablespoons cheese. Bake 12 to 15 minutes or until golden brown.

RISI BISI

MAKES 6 SERVINGS

1½ **cups uncooked converted long grain rice**

¾ **cup chopped onion**

2 **cloves garlic, minced**

2 **cans (about 14 ounces each) chicken broth**

⅓ **cup water**

¾ **teaspoon Italian seasoning**

½ **teaspoon dried basil**

½ **cup frozen peas**

¼ **cup grated Parmesan cheese**

¼ **cup toasted pine nuts (optional)**

SLOW COOKER DIRECTIONS

1. Combine rice, onion and garlic in slow cooker.

2. Bring broth and water to a boil in small saucepan. Stir broth mixture, Italian seasoning and basil into rice mixture in slow cooker. Cover; cook on LOW 2 to 3 hours or until liquid is absorbed.

3. Add peas. Cover; cook on LOW 1 hour. Stir in cheese. Sprinkle with pine nuts, if desired.

DRY-COOKED GREEN BEANS

MAKES 4 SERVINGS

4 **ounces ground pork or turkey**

2 **tablespoons plus 1 teaspoon soy sauce, divided**

2 **tablespoons plus 1 teaspoon rice wine or dry sherry, divided**

½ **teaspoon dark sesame oil**

2 **tablespoons water**

1 **teaspoon sugar**

3 **cups vegetable oil**

1 **pound fresh green beans, trimmed and cut into 2-inch lengths**

1 **tablespoon sliced green onion**

1. Combine pork, 1 teaspoon soy sauce, 1 teaspoon rice wine and sesame oil in medium bowl; mix well. Set aside.

2. Combine water, sugar, remaining 2 tablespoons soy sauce and 2 tablespoons rice wine in small bowl; mix well. Set aside.

3. Heat vegetable oil in wok to 375°F over medium-high heat. Carefully add half of beans; cook 2 to 3 minutes or until beans blister and are crisp-tender. Remove to paper towel-lined plate with slotted spoon to drain. When oil returns to 375°F, repeat with remaining beans.

4. Pour off oil; heat wok over medium-high heat 30 seconds. Add pork mixture; stir-fry about 2 minutes or until well browned. Add beans and soy sauce mixture; cook and stir until heated through. Transfer to serving dish; sprinkle with green onion.

MAKE-AND-TAKE DESSERTS

CIDER-GLAZED PUMPKIN BUNDT CAKES

MAKES 10 CAKES

- 1 **package (about 15 ounces) spice cake mix**
- 1 **can (15 ounces) solid-pack pumpkin**
- 3 **eggs**
- 2/3 **cup water**
- 1/3 **cup vegetable oil**
- 4 **cups plus 2 tablespoons apple cider, divided**
- 16 **whole cloves**
- 1/2 **teaspoon ground cinnamon**
- 1 1/2 **teaspoons cornstarch**

1. Preheat oven to 350°F. Grease and flour 10 mini (1-cup) bundt pan cups.

2. Combine cake mix, pumpkin, eggs, water and oil in large bowl; beat until well blended. Spoon batter evenly into prepared bundt pan cups (about 1/2 cup batter per cup).

3. Bake 30 minutes or until toothpick inserted near centers comes out clean. Cool in pans 15 minutes; invert onto wire racks to cool completely.

4. Meanwhile, combine 4 cups cider, cloves and cinnamon in nonstick skillet; bring to a boil over high heat. Boil 7 minutes or until liquid has reduced to 1 cup. Whisk cornstarch into remaining 2 tablespoons cider in small bowl until smooth. Add to cider mixture; cook and stir until slightly thickened. Remove from heat; cool completely.

5. Remove and discard cloves. Spoon glaze over cakes.

CRANBERRY CRUNCH GELATIN

MAKES 8 SERVINGS

2 **cups boiling water**

2 **packages (4-serving size each) cherry-flavored gelatin**

1 **can (16 ounces) whole berry cranberry sauce**

1½ **cups mini marshmallows**

1 **cup coarsely chopped walnuts**

1. Stir boiling water into gelatin in large bowl 2 minutes or until completely dissolved. Chill about 2 hours or until slightly set.

2. Fold cranberry sauce, marshmallows and walnuts into gelatin mixture. Pour into 6-cup gelatin mold. Cover; refrigerate at least 4 hours or until set. Remove from mold.

LIME & PINEAPPLE SEAFOAM SALAD

MAKES 8 TO 10 SERVINGS

2 **cans (8 ounces each) crushed pineapple in juice**

1 **package (4-serving size) lime gelatin**

1 **cup boiling water**

½ **cup cold water**

1 **package (8 ounces) cream cheese, softened**

¾ **cup coarsely chopped pecans**

⅔ **cup celery slices**

1½ **cups thawed whipped topping**

1. Drain pineapple in sieve. Squeeze pineapple to remove most of juice. Reserve 3 tablespoons juice.

2. Place gelatin in medium bowl; stir in boiling water until gelatin is dissolved. Stir in cold water and reserved 3 tablespoons pineapple juice.

3. Beat cream cheese in large bowl with electric mixer until smooth. Beat in ¼ cup gelatin mixture until blended. Slowly beat in remaining gelatin mixture. Chill 1 hour or until thickened.

4. Stir in pineapple, pecans and celery. Fold in whipped topping. Pour into clear glass serving dish. Chill 2 hours or until set.

PINEAPPLE OATMEAL COOKIES

MAKES ABOUT 4 DOZEN

1 **can (20 oz.) DOLE® Crushed Pineapple**

1½ **cups packed brown sugar**

1 **cup butter or margarine, softened**

1 **egg**

3 **cups old fashioned or quick cooking oats**

2 **cups all-purpose flour**

1 **teaspoon baking powder**

1 **teaspoon ground cinnamon**

½ **teaspoon salt**

1 **cup DOLE® Seedless or Golden Raisins**

1 **cup chopped almonds, toasted (optional)**

DRAIN pineapple well; reserve ½ cup juice.

BEAT sugar and butter until light and fluffy in large bowl. Beat in egg, crushed pineapple and reserved juice.

COMBINE oats, flour, baking powder, cinnamon, salt, raisins and almonds in medium bowl. Stir into pineapple mixture.

DROP by heaping tablespoonfuls onto greased cookie sheets. Shape with back of spoon.

BAKE at 350°F., 20 to 25 minutes or until golden. Cool on wire racks.

BERRY BUNDT CAKE

MAKES 12 SERVINGS

2 cups all-purpose flour

1 tablespoon baking powder

1 teaspoon baking soda

¼ teaspoon salt

1 cup sugar

¾ cup buttermilk*

2 eggs

¼ cup vegetable oil

2 cups frozen unsweetened raspberries

2 cups frozen unsweetened blueberries

If you don't have buttermilk, substitute 2¼ teaspoons vinegar or lemon juice plus enough milk to equal ¾ cup. Let stand 5 minutes.

1. Preheat oven to 350°F. Spray 6-cup bundt pan with nonstick cooking spray.

2. Combine flour, baking powder, baking soda and salt in large bowl; mix well. Whisk sugar, buttermilk, eggs and oil in medium bowl until well blended. Add sugar mixture to flour mixture; stir just until moistened. Fold in raspberries and blueberries. Pour into prepared pan.

3. Bake 1 hour or until toothpick inserted near center comes out clean. Cool completely in pan on wire rack.

CHEESECAKE 5 WAYS

MAKES 10 TO 12 SERVINGS

CRUMB CRUST (recipe follows)

3 **packages (8 ounces each) cream cheese, softened**

¾ **cup sugar**

3 **eggs**

1 **teaspoon vanilla extract**

1. Prepare CRUMB CRUST. Heat oven to 350°F.

2. Beat cream cheese and sugar in large bowl until smooth. Add eggs, one at a time, beating well after each addition. Stir in vanilla. Pour into prepared crust.

3. Bake 45 to 50 minutes or until almost set.* Remove from oven to wire rack. With knife, loosen cake from side of pan. Cool completely; remove side of pan.

4. Cover; refrigerate several hours or until chilled. Just before serving, garnish as desired. Cover and refrigerate leftover cheesecake.

Cheesecakes are less likely to crack if baked in a water bath.

CRUMB CRUST: Heat oven to 350°F. Stir together 1 cup graham cracker crumbs and 2 tablespoons sugar in small bowl; blend in ¼ cup (½ stick) melted butter or margarine, mixing well. Press mixture onto bottom and ½ inch up side of 9-inch springform pan. Bake 8 to 10 minutes. Cool.

CHOCOLATE CHEESECAKE: Increase sugar to 1¼ cups and add ⅓ cup HERSHEY'®S Cocoa. Increase vanilla extract to 1½ teaspoons.

TOFFEE BITS CHEESECAKE: Prepare cheesecake as directed. Stir 1⅓ cups (8-ounce package) HEATH® BITS 'O BRICKLE® Toffee Bits into batter.

CHOCOLATE CHIP CHEESECAKE: Prepare cheesecake as directed. Stir 1 to 1½ cups HERSHEY'®S Mini Chips® Semi-Sweet Chocolate into batter.

MOCHA CHEESECAKE: Prepare Chocolate Cheesecake, using HERSHEY'®S SPECIAL DARK® Cocoa. Add 1½ teaspoons powdered instant coffee to batter.

MOCHA TOFFEE WITH CHOCOLATE CHIPS CHEESECAKE: Prepare Mocha Cheesecake as directed. Stir ¾ cup HEATH® BITS 'O BRICKLE® Toffee Bits and ¾ cup HERSHEY'®S Mini Chips® Semi-Sweet Chocolate into batter.

RAINBOW POKE CAKE

MAKES 12 TO 15 SERVINGS

1 package (about 15 ounces) white cake mix, plus ingredients to prepare mix

Gel food coloring (6 colors)

1 package (4-serving size) orange gelatin

1 cup boiling water

½ cup cold water

1 container (8 ounces) frozen whipped topping, thawed

½ cup colored nonpareils

1. Prepare cake mix according to package directions. Divide batter evenly into six small bowls. Add one food coloring to each individual bowl until desired shade is reached.

2. Prop one end of 13×9-inch pan on wooden spoon; alternately pour batters in crosswise lines into pan. Bake according to package directions; cool completely.

3. Poke holes in cake at ½-inch intervals with fork. Combine gelatin and boiling water in small bowl; stir until gelatin is dissolved. Stir in cold water. Cool gelatin slightly; pour over cake. Top cake with whipped topping and nonpareils.

STRAWBERRY RHUBARB PIE

MAKES 8 SERVINGS

3 cups sliced fresh or frozen rhubarb, divided

½ cup unsweetened white grape juice

2 tablespoons cornstarch

1 teaspoon ground cinnamon

¼ teaspoon ground nutmeg

¼ teaspoon salt

1 pint fresh strawberries, sliced (about 3½ cups)

¾ cup strawberry fruit spread, divided

Pastry for double-crust 9-inch pie

1 egg yolk, lightly beaten

1 tablespoon sour cream

1. Preheat oven to 450°F.

2. Combine 2 cups rhubarb and grape juice in medium saucepan. Bring to a boil over medium heat. Reduce heat to low. Simmer, uncovered, until rhubarb is tender, 8 to 10 minutes for fresh, or 5 minutes for frozen; drain.

3. Combine cornstarch, cinnamon, nutmeg and salt in medium bowl; mix well. Add strawberries; toss to coat. Stir in cooked rhubarb and ½ cup fruit spread. Stir in remaining 1 cup rhubarb.

4. Roll out half of pastry to 11-inch circle; place in 9-inch pie plate. Trim pastry and flute edges, sealing to edge of pie plate. Fill shell with fruit mixture; dot with remaining ¼ cup fruit spread. Roll out remaining pastry to 10-inch circle. Cut into ½-inch wide strips. Form into lattice design over fruit.

5. Combine egg yolk and sour cream in small bowl; mix until well blended. Brush over pastry. Bake 10 minutes. *Reduce oven temperature to 350°F. Bake 30 minutes or until pastry is golden brown and filling is hot and bubbly.* Cool on wire rack. Serve warm or at room temperature.

Pie may be covered loosely with foil during last 30 minutes of baking to prevent overbrowning, if desired.

LEMON SQUARES

MAKES 2 TO 3 DOZEN BARS

CRUST

1 cup (2 sticks) butter, softened

½ cup granulated sugar

½ teaspoon salt

2 cups all-purpose flour

FILLING

3 cups granulated sugar

1 cup all-purpose flour

4 eggs plus 2 egg yolks, at room temperature

⅔ cup fresh lemon juice

2 tablespoons grated lemon peel

½ teaspoon baking powder

Powdered sugar

1. Beat butter, ½ cup granulated sugar and salt in large bowl with electric mixer at medium speed until light and fluffy. Add 2 cups flour; mix on low speed just until blended.

2. Press dough into 13×9-inch baking pan, building edges up ½ inch on all sides. Refrigerate 20 minutes or until slightly firm.

3. Preheat oven to 350°F. Bake 15 to 20 minutes or until very lightly browned. Cool on wire rack.

4. Whisk 3 cups granulated sugar, 1 cup flour, eggs and egg yolks, lemon juice, lemon peel and baking powder in large bowl until well blended. Pour over crust.

5. Bake 30 to 35 minutes until filling is set. Cool completely in pan on wire rack. Cut into squares; sprinkle with powdered sugar.

OLD-FASHIONED APPLE PIE

MAKES 8 TO 10 SERVINGS

REYNOLDS® Parchment Paper

Pastry for 9-inch deep dish, double crust pie, prepared

4 to 5 cups (3 pounds) tart cooking apples, peeled, cored and sliced

1¼ cups sugar

⅓ cup flour

1 teaspoon ground cinnamon

1 tablespoon butter

2 teaspoons milk

½ teaspoon sugar

PREHEAT oven to 350°F. Roll out half of pastry to ⅛-inch thickness on a sheet of REYNOLDS® Parchment Paper. Place in 9-inch deep dish pie plate; set aside. Combine apples, sugar, flour and cinnamon in a large bowl; mix to coat apples. Spoon mixture evenly into pie crust; top with butter.

ROLL remaining pastry for top crust to ⅛-inch thickness on a floured sheet of REYNOLDS® Parchment Paper. Cut into ½-inch strips. Arrange in lattice design over fruit. Brush pastry lightly with milk; sprinkle with sugar.

BAKE 45 to 50 minutes or until crust is golden brown. Serve warm.

CHOCOLATE CHIP COOKIE BARS

MAKES 16 (2X3-INCH) BARS

½ cup (1 stick) butter, softened

½ cup vegetable shortening

¾ cup granulated sugar

¾ cup packed brown sugar

2 eggs

1 teaspoon vanilla

2½ cups all-purpose flour

1 teaspoon baking soda

1 teaspoon salt

2 cups (12 ounces) semisweet chocolate chips

1 cup chopped pecans or walnuts

1. Preheat oven to 375°F. Grease or coat 13×9-inch baking dish with nonstick cooking spray; set aside.

2. Beat butter, shortening, granulated sugar and brown sugar in large bowl with electric mixer at medium speed 3 minutes or until creamy. Add eggs and vanilla. Beat 2 minutes. Reduce speed to low. Beat in flour, baking soda and salt. Fold in chips and pecans.

3. Spread dough evenly in prepared baking dish. Bake 20 minutes or until golden brown and firm to the touch. Cool completely.

VARIATIONS: Substitute peanut butter chips, milk chocolate chips or raspberry-flavored chips for half or all of the semisweet chocolate chips.

SPICED PEACH PIE

MAKES 8 SERVINGS

Double-Crust Pie Pastry (recipe follows)

1 egg, separated

2 tablespoons cornstarch

2 teaspoons ground cinnamon

$1/2$ teaspoon ground nutmeg

$1/8$ teaspoon salt

$1/2$ cup unsweetened apple juice concentrate

1 teaspoon vanilla

5 cups sliced peeled fresh peaches or frozen unsweetened sliced peaches, thawed and well drained

1 tablespoon butter

1 teaspoon cold water

1. Prepare Double-Crust Pie Pastry. Preheat oven to 400°F. Roll out one disc pastry on floured surface into 11-inch circle. Line 9-inch pie plate with pastry. Beat egg white in small bowl until frothy; brush over pastry.

2. Combine cornstarch, cinnamon, nutmeg and salt in large bowl; mix well. Stir in juice concentrate and vanilla. Add peaches; toss lightly to coat. Spoon into crust; dot with butter.

3. Roll out remaining disc pastry into 10-inch circle. Cut into ½-inch-wide strips. Arrange in lattice design over peaches. Seal and flute edge. Whisk egg yolk and water in small bowl; brush over pastry.

4. Bake 50 minutes or until pastry is golden brown and filling is thick and bubbly.* Cool on wire rack. Serve warm, at room temperature or chilled.

Cover pie loosely with foil after 30 minutes of baking to prevent overbrowning, if necessary.

DOUBLE-CRUST PIE PASTRY: Combine 2½ cups all-purpose flour, 1 teaspoon salt and 1 teaspoon sugar in large bowl. Cut in 1 cup (2 sticks) cubed unsalted butter with pastry blender or two knives until mixture resembles coarse crumbs. Drizzle ⅓ cup water over flour mixture, 2 tablespoons at a time, stirring just until dough comes together. Form each half into a disc; wrap in plastic wrap. Refrigerate 30 minutes.

CHOCOLATE CHIP SANDWICH COOKIES

MAKES 16 SANDWICH COOKIES

3/4 cup plus 1/3 cup packed brown sugar

1/2 cup (1 stick) butter, softened

1 egg

1 teaspoon vanilla

3/4 teaspoon baking soda

1/2 teaspoon salt

1 3/4 cups all-purpose flour

3 cups semisweet chocolate chips, divided

6 tablespoons whipping cream

1. Preheat oven to 350°F. Line cookie sheets with parchment paper.

2. Beat brown sugar and butter in large bowl with electric mixer at medium speed 5 minutes or until light and fluffy. Add egg and vanilla; beat until well blended. Beat in baking soda and salt. Slowly add flour, beating at low speed until blended. Stir in 1½ cups chocolate chips.

3. Drop heaping tablespoonfuls of dough 2 inches apart onto prepared cookie sheets. Bake about 10 minutes or until cookies are just beginning to brown around edges but are still very soft in center. (Cookies will look underbaked.) Cool on cookie sheets 5 minutes; remove to wire racks to cool completely.

4. While cookies are baking, prepare ganache filling. Heat cream to a simmer in microwave oven or on stovetop. Add remaining 1½ cups chocolate chips to cream; let stand 1 minute. Stir mixture until smooth. Refrigerate 1 hour, stirring occasionally. (Filling should be thick enough to spread and still be shiny when stirred.)

5. Spread heaping tablespoonful of chocolate filling onto bottoms of half the cookies. Top with remaining cookies.

CHOCOLATE PRETZEL COOKIES

MAKES 4 DOZEN COOKIES

1 cup (2 sticks) butter, softened

3/4 cup granulated sugar

1/2 cup unsweetened cocoa powder

1 egg

1 teaspoon vanilla

2 cups cake flour

1 teaspoon coarse salt, plus additional for garnish

4 ounces white chocolate, chopped

Pearl sugar

1. Beat butter and granulated sugar in large bowl with electric mixer until light. Add cocoa powder, egg and vanilla; beat until well blended. Stir in flour and 1 teaspoon salt until well blended. Shape dough into a disc; wrap in plastic wrap. Refrigerate 1 hour or until firm.

2. Preheat oven to 350°F. Line cookie sheets with parchment paper. Roll tablespoonfuls of dough into 12-inch ropes; shape into pretzels and place on prepared cookie sheets 2 inches apart. Bake 7 to 8 minutes or until firm. Cool on cookie sheets 5 minutes. Remove to wire racks; cool completely.

3. Place cookies on parchment paper. Melt white chocolate according to package directions. Drizzle over cookies; sprinkle with additional salt and pearl sugar. Let stand until white chocolate is completely set.

AUNT RUTH'S FAVORITE WHITE CAKE

MAKES ONE 2-LAYER CAKE

1 package (about 18 ounces) white cake mix

1¼ cups water

3 eggs

2 tablespoons vegetable oil

1 teaspoon vanilla

½ teaspoon almond extract

Creamy White Frosting (recipe follows)

1. Preheat oven to 350°F. Grease and flour two 9-inch round cake pans.

2. Beat cake mix, water, eggs and oil in large mixing bowl with electric mixer at medium speed until well blended. Add vanilla and almond extract; beat until well blended. Divide batter evenly between prepared pans.

3. Bake 30 to 35 minutes or until toothpick inserted near the centers comes out clean. Cool on wire racks 10 minutes. Remove cakes from pans to racks; cool completely.

4. Prepare Creamy White Frosting. Fill and frost cake with frosting.

CREAMY WHITE FROSTING | MAKES ABOUT 2 CUPS

3 tablespoons all-purpose flour

1 cup milk

1 cup (2 sticks) butter, softened

1 cup powdered sugar

1 teaspoon vanilla

1. Combine flour and milk in medium saucepan. Bring to a boil over medium heat. Cook and stir 1 to 2 minutes or until thickened. Cool.

2. Beat butter in large bowl until creamy. Add powdered sugar; beat until fluffy. Blend in vanilla. Add flour mixture; beat until thick and smooth.

CHOCOLATE DREAM BARS

MAKES 2 TO 3 DOZEN BARS

2¼ cups all-purpose flour, divided

1 cup (2 sticks) butter, softened

¾ cup powdered sugar, plus additional for garnish

⅓ cup unsweetened cocoa powder

½ teaspoon salt

2 cups granulated sugar

4 eggs, lightly beaten

4 ounces unsweetened chocolate, melted

1. Preheat oven to 350°F. Line 13×9-inch baking pan with parchment paper.

2. Beat 2 cups flour, butter, ¾ cup powdered sugar, cocoa and salt in large bowl with electric mixer at low speed until blended. Beat at medium speed until well blended and stiff dough forms. Press firmly into prepared pan. Bake 15 to 20 minutes or just until set. *Do not overbake.*

3. Meanwhile, combine remaining ¼ cup flour and granulated sugar in large bowl. Add eggs and melted chocolate; beat with electric mixer at medium-high speed until well blended. Pour over crust.

4. Bake 25 minutes or until center is firm to the touch. Cool completely in pan on wire rack. Sprinkle with additional powdered sugar, if desired. Cut into bars.

HONEY LIME FRUIT TOSS

MAKES 7 SERVINGS

1 **can (20 oz.) DOLE®
   Pineapple Chunks**

1 **can (11 or 15 oz.) DOLE®
   Mandarin Oranges, drained**

1 **large DOLE® Banana, sliced**

1 **DOLE® Kiwi fruit, peeled,
   halved and sliced**

1 **cup quartered DOLE® Fresh
   or Frozen Strawberries**

¼ **teaspoon grated lime peel
   (optional)**

2 **tablespoons fresh lime juice**

1 **tablespoon honey**

DRAIN pineapple; reserve ¼ cup juice.

COMBINE pineapple chunks, mandarin oranges, banana, kiwi fruit and strawberries in large serving bowl.

STIR together reserved pineapple juice, lime peel, lime juice and honey in small bowl. Pour over salad; toss to coat.

CHUNKY OATMEAL RAISIN COOKIES

MAKES ABOUT 4 DOZEN COOKIES

1 package (about 18 ounces) yellow cake mix

1½ cups old-fashioned oats

½ cup all-purpose flour

2 teaspoons ground cinnamon

½ cup packed brown sugar

2 eggs

1 teaspoon vanilla

1 cup (2 sticks) unsalted butter, melted

1 cup raisins

1 cup walnut pieces, toasted

1. Preheat oven to 375°F. Line cookie sheets with parchment paper.

2. Combine cake mix, oats, flour and cinnamon in medium bowl. Beat brown sugar, eggs and vanilla in large bowl with electric mixer at medium speed until blended. Beat in dry ingredients and butter until combined. Stir in raisins and walnuts.

3. Drop dough by tablespoonfuls 2 inches apart onto prepared cookie sheets. Bake 14 to 16 minutes or until bottoms are golden brown. Cool on cookie sheets 2 minutes. Remove to wire racks; cool completely.

PUMPKIN CHEESECAKE

MAKES 12 SERVINGS

CRUST

18	graham crackers (2 sleeves)
1/4	cup sugar
1/8	teaspoon salt
1/2	cup (1 stick) butter, melted

FILLING

1	can (15 ounces) solid-pack pumpkin
1/4	cup sour cream
2	teaspoons vanilla
2	teaspoons ground cinnamon, plus additional for garnish
1	teaspoon ground ginger
1/4	teaspoon salt
1/4	teaspoon ground cloves
4	packages (8 ounces each) cream cheese, softened
1 3/4	cups sugar
5	eggs
	Whipped cream

1. Line bottom of 9-inch springform with parchment paper. Spray bottom and side of pan with nonstick cooking spray. Wrap bottom and side of pan with heavy-duty foil.

2. For crust, place graham crackers in food processor; pulse until fine crumbs form. Add 1/4 cup sugar and 1/8 teaspoon salt; pulse to blend. Add butter; pulse until crumbs are moistened and mixture is well blended. Press crumb mixture onto bottom and all the way up side of prepared pan in thin layer. Refrigerate at least 20 minutes. Preheat oven to 350°F. Bake crust 12 minutes; cool on wire rack. Bring large saucepan of water to a boil.

3. For filling, whisk pumpkin, sour cream, vanilla, 2 teaspoons cinnamon, ginger, 1/4 teaspoon salt and cloves in medium bowl until well blended. Beat cream cheese and 1 3/4 cups sugar in large bowl with electric mixer at medium speed until smooth and well blended. With mixer running, beat in eggs, one at a time, until blended. Scrape side of bowl. Add pumpkin mixture; beat at medium speed until well blended. Pour into crust. Place springform pan in large roasting pan; place in oven. Carefully add boiling water to roasting pan to come about halfway up side of springform pan.

4. Bake 1 hour 15 minutes or until top is set and lightly browned. Remove cheesecake from water; remove foil. Cool to room temperature in pan on wire rack. Run small thin spatula around edge of pan to loosen crust. (Do not remove side of pan.) Cover with plastic wrap; refrigerate 8 hours or overnight. Garnish with whipped cream and additional cinnamon.

ACKNOWLEDGMENTS

The publisher would like to thank the companies and organization listed below for
the use of their recipes and photographs in this publication.

ACH Food Companies, Inc.

The Beef Checkoff

Bob Evans®

Campbell Soup Company

Cream of Wheat® Cereal, A Division of B&G
    Foods North America, Inc.

Dole Food Company, Inc.

Hormel Foods, The Makers of Hormel® Cure
    81® Ham

Mizkan America, Inc.

McCormick®

Ortega®, A Division of B&G Foods North
    America, Inc.

Pinnacle Foods

Polaner®, A Division of B&G Foods North
    America, Inc.

Reckitt Benckiser LLC

Recipes courtesy of the Reynolds Kitchens

Riviana Foods Inc.

2018 Sunbeam Products, Inc. doing business
    as Jarden Consumer Solutions.

Unilever

Upfield

METRIC CONVERSION CHART

VOLUME MEASUREMENTS (dry)

1/8 teaspoon = 0.5 mL
1/4 teaspoon = 1 mL
1/2 teaspoon = 2 mL
3/4 teaspoon = 4 mL
1 teaspoon = 5 mL
1 tablespoon = 15 mL
2 tablespoons = 30 mL
1/4 cup = 60 mL
1/3 cup = 75 mL
1/2 cup = 125 mL
2/3 cup = 150 mL
3/4 cup = 175 mL
1 cup = 250 mL
2 cups = 1 pint = 500 mL
3 cups = 750 mL
4 cups = 1 quart = 1 L

VOLUME MEASUREMENTS (fluid)

1 fluid ounce (2 tablespoons) = 30 mL
4 fluid ounces (1/2 cup) = 125 mL
8 fluid ounces (1 cup) = 250 mL
12 fluid ounces (1 1/2 cups) = 375 mL
16 fluid ounces (2 cups) = 500 mL

WEIGHTS (mass)

1/2 ounce = 15 g
1 ounce = 30 g
3 ounces = 90 g
4 ounces = 120 g
8 ounces = 225 g
10 ounces = 285 g
12 ounces = 360 g
16 ounces = 1 pound = 450 g

DIMENSIONS

1/16 inch = 2 mm
1/8 inch = 3 mm
1/4 inch = 6 mm
1/2 inch = 1.5 cm
3/4 inch = 2 cm
1 inch = 2.5 cm

OVEN TEMPERATURES

250°F = 120°C
275°F = 140°C
300°F = 150°C
325°F = 160°C
350°F = 180°C
375°F = 190°C
400°F = 200°C
425°F = 220°C
450°F = 230°C

BAKING PAN SIZES

Utensil	Size in Inches/Quarts	Metric Volume	Size in Centimeters
Baking or Cake Pan (square or rectangular)	8×8×2	2 L	20×20×5
	9×9×2	2.5 L	23×23×5
	12×8×2	3 L	30×20×5
	13×9×2	3.5 L	33×23×5
Loaf Pan	8×4×3	1.5 L	20×10×7
	9×5×3	2 L	23×13×7
Round Layer Cake Pan	8×1½	1.2 L	20×4
	9×1½	1.5 L	23×4
Pie Plate	8×1¼	750 mL	20×3
	9×1¼	1 L	23×3
Baking Dish or Casserole	1 quart	1 L	—
	1½ quart	1.5 L	—
	2 quart	2 L	—